WORKING PAPERS FOR EXERCISES AND PROBLEMS
VOLUME 2: CHAPTERS 19–27

PRINCIPLES OF ACCOUNTING
2002e

Belverd E. Needles, Jr.
DePaul University

Marian Powers
Northwestern University

Susan V. Crosson
Santa Fe Community College, Florida

HOUGHTON MIFFLIN COMPANY   BOSTON   NEW YORK

Senior Sponsoring Editor: Bonnie Binkert
Senior Development Editor: Margaret M. Kearney
Associate Project Editor: Claudine Bellanton
Senior Manufacturing Coordinator: Priscilla J. Bailey
Marketing Manager: Steven Mikels

Copyright © 2002 by Houghton Mifflin Company. All rights reserved.

No part of this work may be reproduced or transmitted in any form or by any means, electronic or mechanical, including photocopying or recording, or by any information storage or retrieval system without the prior written permission of Houghton Mifflin Company unless such copying is expressly permitted by federal copyright law. Address inquiries to College Permissions, Houghton Mifflin Company, 222 Berkeley Street, Boston, MA 02116-3764.

Printed in the U.S.A.

ISBN: 0-618-12429-2

123456789-POO-05 04 03 02 01

NOTE TO STUDENTS

This book contains Working Papers to be used in preparing solutions to all Exercises, Problems, and selected cases in Chapters 19–27 of *Principles of Accounting,* 2002e. The Working Papers are designed to simplify your work; appropriate forms for computational assignments for each exercise and problem are provided, and some preliminary information has been printed to help you get started. Items requiring extensive written responses should be word processed or submitted on lined paper.

We have occasionally provided hints on the placement of data. This is usually done only once on a page. Students can infer from these hints where to enter subsequent data on that page so that it can be displayed and calculated correctly.

Accounting Format Guide

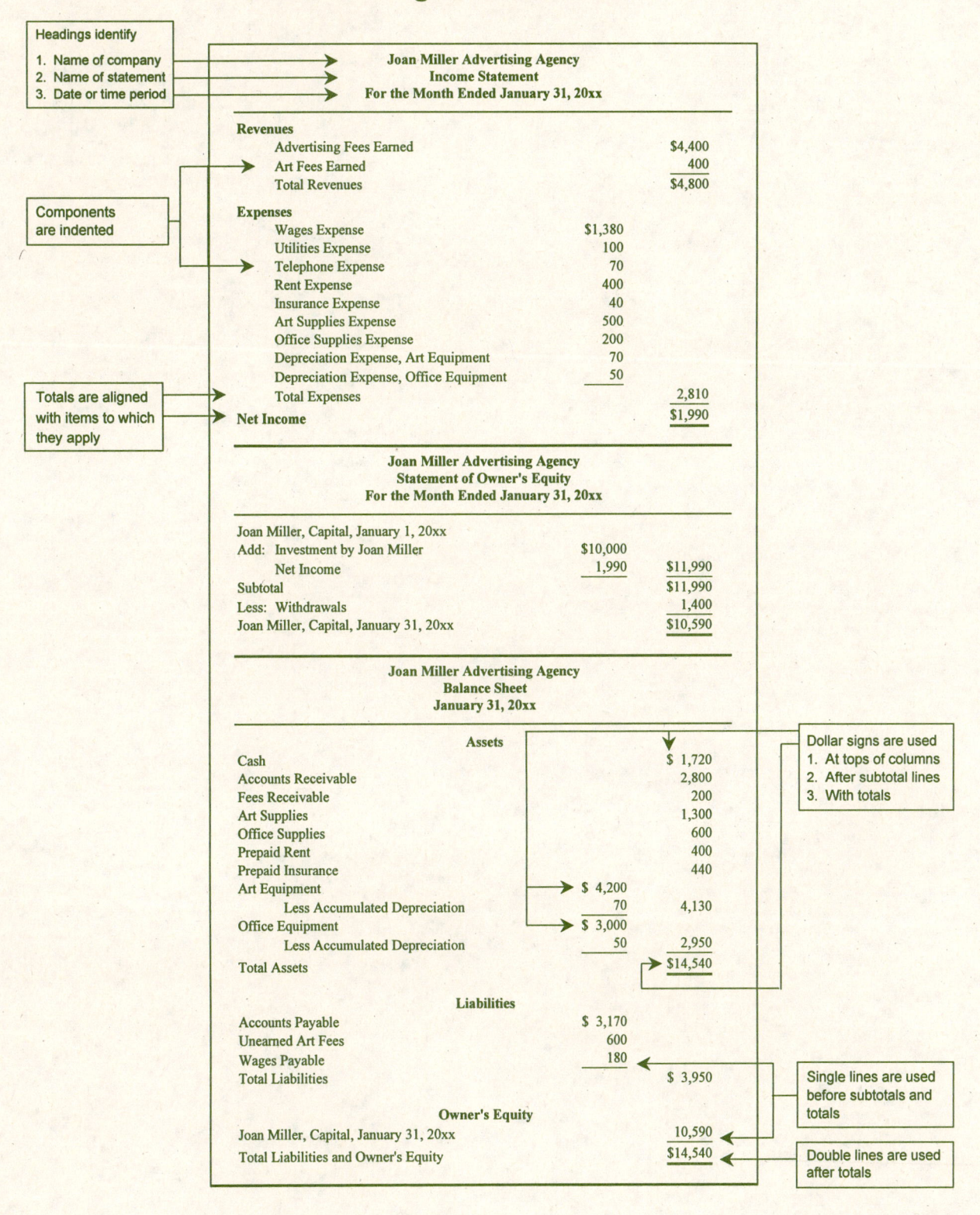

Headings identify
1. Name of company
2. Name of statement
3. Date or time period

Joan Miller Advertising Agency
Income Statement
For the Month Ended January 31, 20xx

Revenues
Advertising Fees Earned		$4,400
Art Fees Earned		400
Total Revenues		$4,800

Components are indented

Expenses
Wages Expense	$1,380	
Utilities Expense	100	
Telephone Expense	70	
Rent Expense	400	
Insurance Expense	40	
Art Supplies Expense	500	
Office Supplies Expense	200	
Depreciation Expense, Art Equipment	70	
Depreciation Expense, Office Equipment	50	
Total Expenses		2,810
Net Income		**$1,990**

Totals are aligned with items to which they apply

Joan Miller Advertising Agency
Statement of Owner's Equity
For the Month Ended January 31, 20xx

Joan Miller, Capital, January 1, 20xx		
Add: Investment by Joan Miller	$10,000	
Net Income	1,990	$11,990
Subtotal		$11,990
Less: Withdrawals		1,400
Joan Miller, Capital, January 31, 20xx		$10,590

Joan Miller Advertising Agency
Balance Sheet
January 31, 20xx

Assets
Cash		$ 1,720
Accounts Receivable		2,800
Fees Receivable		200
Art Supplies		1,300
Office Supplies		600
Prepaid Rent		400
Prepaid Insurance		440
Art Equipment	$ 4,200	
Less Accumulated Depreciation	70	4,130
Office Equipment	$ 3,000	
Less Accumulated Depreciation	50	2,950
Total Assets		$14,540

Dollar signs are used
1. At tops of columns
2. After subtotal lines
3. With totals

Liabilities
Accounts Payable	$ 3,170	
Unearned Art Fees	600	
Wages Payable	180	
Total Liabilities		$ 3,950

Owner's Equity
Joan Miller, Capital, January 31, 20xx		10,590
Total Liabilities and Owner's Equity		$14,540

Single lines are used before subtotals and totals

Double lines are used after totals

Chapter 19, SE 1.

1.
2.
3.
4.
5.
6.
7.
8.

Chapter 19, SE 2.

1.
2.
3.
4.
5.
6.

Chapter 19, SE 3.

Chapter 19, SE 4.

Chapter 19, SE 5.

Chapter 19, SE 6.

1.
2.
3.
4.
5.
6.

Chapter 19, SE 7.

Chapter 19, SE 8.

Chapter 19, SE 9.

1.
2.
3.

Chapter 19, SE 10.

Chapter 19, E 1.

Chapter 19, E 2.

1.		6.	
2.		7.	
3.		8.	
4.		9.	
5.		10.	

Chapter 19, E 3.

CFO 1:	
CFO 2:	
CFO 3:	
CFO 4:	

Chapter 19, E 4.

1.	
2.	
3.	
4.	
5.	

Chapter 19, E 5.

	Elway	Mahoney	Fencereaux	Pfister	Onski	Mantero
Hours worked						
Square yards of sod planted						
Square yards that should have been planted (500 yd/person/hr × hr worked)						
Yards under (over) target						
Percent under (over) target						

Results of the analysis:

Chapter 19, E 6.

Day	Maximum Number of Rejected Cookies Allowed	Actual Number of Rejected Cookies	Variance Under (Over) Allowed Maximum
Monday			
Tuesday			
Wednesday			
Thursday			
Friday			
Total			
Daily Average			

Chapter 19, E 7.

CN and CP Average Weekly Output

Computer	Weeks									
	One	Two	Three	Four	Five	Six	Seven	Eight	Nine	Ten
CN										
CP										
Total										
Divide by 2										
Average Output										

Comparison Analysis

Computer	Weeks									
	One	Two	Three	Four	Five	Six	Seven	Eight	Nine	Ten
CM										
Average Output										
Difference										

New Computer	> or <	Additional Memory

Chapter 19, E 8.

Chapter 19, E 9.

1.	6.
2.	7.
3.	8.
4.	9.
5.	10.

Chapter 19, E 10.

1.
2.
3.
4.
5.
6.
7.
8.
9.

Chapter 19, E 11.

1.
2.
3.

Chapter 19, E 12.

1.
2.
3.

Chapter 19, E 13.

1.
2.
3.

Chapter 19, E 14.

1.
2.
3.

Chapter 19, E 15.

Chapter 19, P 1.

1. Analysis comparing maximum and actual numbers of rejected candy canes prepared

Week 3, 20x4	Maximum Number of Rejected Candy Canes Allowed	Actual Number of Rejected Candy Canes	Variance Under (Over) Allowed Maximum
Monday			
Tuesday			
Wednesday			
Thursday			
Friday			
Total for the Week			
Daily Average			

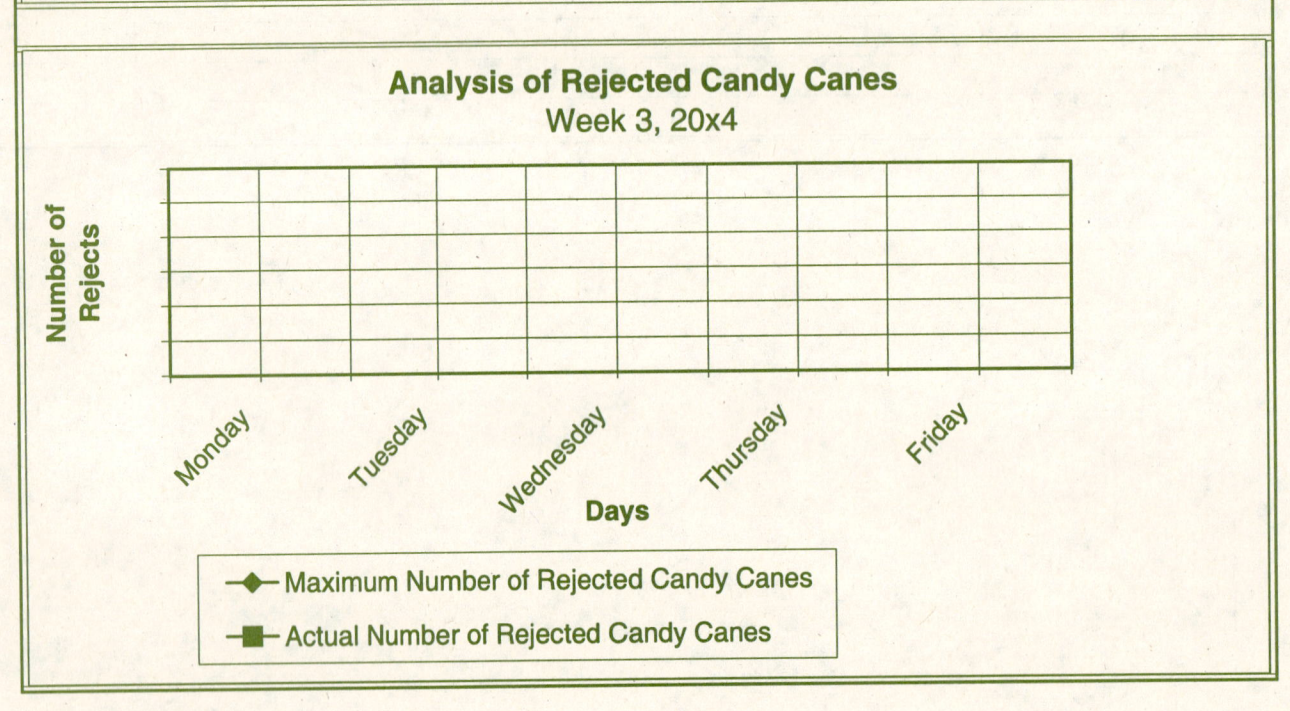

Analysis of Rejected Candy Canes
Week 3, 20x4

Number of Rejects (y-axis) vs *Days* (x-axis: Monday, Tuesday, Wednesday, Thursday, Friday)

♦ Maximum Number of Rejected Candy Canes
■ Actual Number of Rejected Candy Canes

Chapter 19, P 1. (Continued)

2. Analysis comparing number of rejects for each category for Week 1 and Week 3 prepared

	Reasons for Rejects Week 1, 20x4	Reasons for Rejects Week 3, 20x4	Decrease (Increase) in Number of Rejects
Ingredients			
Shaping			
Cooking Time			
Total			

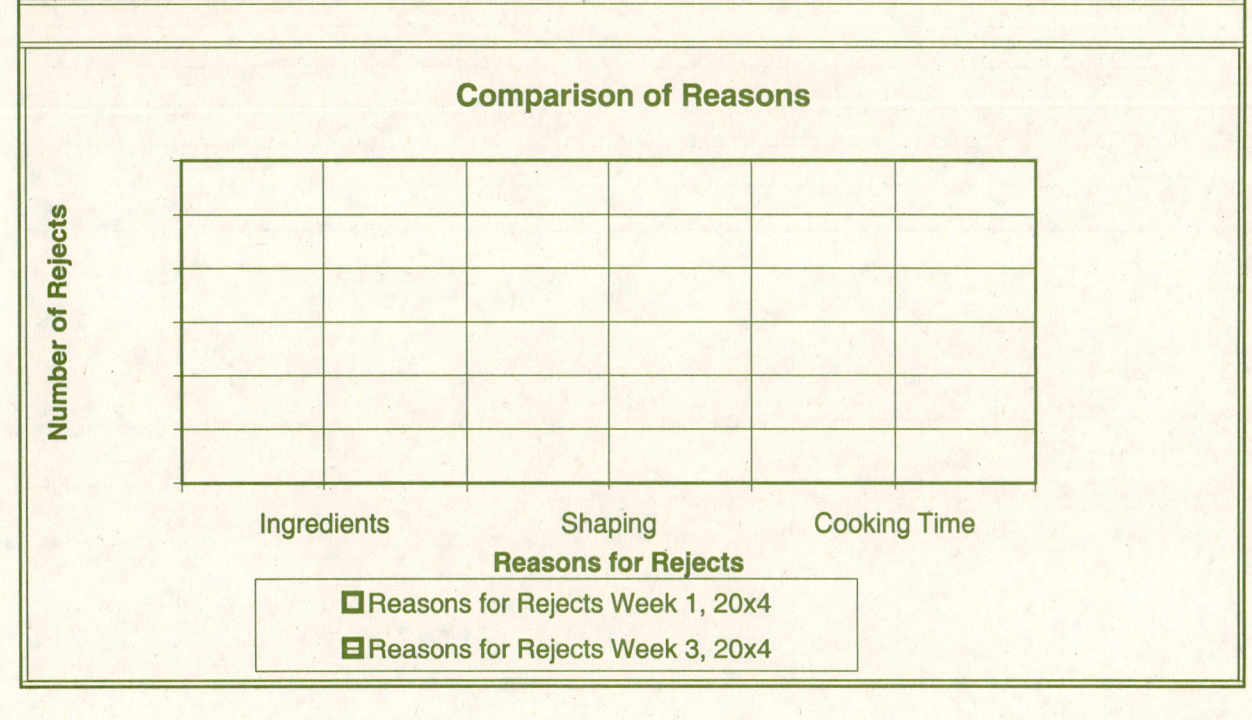

Comparison of Reasons

Number of Rejects (y-axis)

Reasons for Rejects (x-axis): Ingredients, Shaping, Cooking Time

☐ Reasons for Rejects Week 1, 20x4
☒ Reasons for Rejects Week 3, 20x4

Chapter 19, P 1. (Continued)

3. Success in increasing the quality of candy discussed

Chapter 19, P 2.

1. **Average weekly check-sorting output of all machines except Machine BD computed**

Machine	Weeks							
	One	Two	Three	Four	Five	Six	Seven	Eight
AA								
AB								
AC								
AD								
AE								
BA								
BB								
BC								
BE								
Total								
Divided by 9	9	9	9	9	9	9	9	9
Average output								

2. **Comparison of the weekly check-sorting output from Machine BD with the average weekly output from other machines**

Machine	Weeks							
	One	Two	Three	Four	Five	Six	Seven	Eight
BD								
Average output								
Difference								
Percentage change								

Chapter 19, P 2. (Continued)

3. Alternatives discussed

4. Recommendation reevaluated assuming two attachments

5. Recommendation reevaluated assuming three attachments

Chapter 19, P 3.

1. Types of needed information identified

2. The four *W*s considered

   a. Why prepare the report?

   b. What information should be included in the report?

   c. For whom is the report being prepared? To whom will the report be distributed?

   d. When is the report due?

Chapter 19, P 3. (Continued)

3. Report format designed

<table>
<tr><td colspan="7" align="center">Rakes Etc., Inc.
Summary of Plants and Trees for Retail Lawn and Garden Center
Analysis by Location
—Date—</td></tr>
<tr><td>**Location**</td><td colspan="6">**Boston, Massachusetts**</td></tr>
<tr><td></td><td></td><td></td><td></td><td></td><td></td><td></td></tr>
<tr><td></td><td></td><td></td><td></td><td></td><td></td><td></td></tr>
<tr><td></td><td></td><td></td><td></td><td></td><td></td><td></td></tr>
</table>

(List continues with other possible plants and trees.)

(Similar analyses for each location would follow.)

Chapter 19, P 4.

1. Accounts in manufacturing and merchandising organizations identified

a.

b.

2. Key figures calculated

a.	Gross Margin	=	Operating Expenses	+	
		=		+	
		=			
b.	Cost of Goods Sold	=		−	Gross Margin
		=		−	
		=			
c.	Cost of Goods Available for Sale	=	Cost of Goods Sold	+	
		=		+	
		=			
d.	Cost of Goods Manufactured	=		−	Finished Goods Inventory, 12/31/x5
		=		−	
		=			

Chapter 19, P 5.

1. Missing data for a merchandising organization calculated

Note: Items are listed in the suggested order of solution.

First Quarter:

a.	Gross Margin	=	Sales	−					
b.	Net Cost of Purchases	=							
c.	Operating Expenses	=		−	Net Income				
d.	Cost of Goods Available for Sale	=		+	Beginning Merchandise Inventory				
e.		=		+		−	Cost of Goods Sold		
f.	Ending Merchandise Inventory	=	Sales	−	Gross Margin	−			
g.	Beginning Merchandise Inventory	=		−		−	Cost of Goods Available for Sale		

Second Quarter:

e.	Sales	=	Gross Margin	+					
f.	Ending Merchandise Inventory	=		−					
g.	Beginning Merchandise Inventory	=	Cost of Goods Available for Sale	−	Cost of Goods Sold				=

Chapter 19, P 5. (Continued)

Third Quarter:

h. Beginning Merchandise Inventory + _____ = Cost of Goods Available for Sale

i. _____ − Operating Expenses = Net Income

j. Sales − _____ = Cost of Goods Sold

Fourth Quarter:

l. _____ + _____ = Gross Margin

k. Sales + Gross Margin = _____

m. Ending Merchandise Inventory − _____ = Cost of Goods Sold

n. Net Cost of Purchases − _____ = Cost of Goods Available for Sale

Chapter 19, P 5. (Continued)

2. Missing data for a manufacturing organization calculated

First Quarter:

a.	Sales	=		+		
b.	Beginning Finished Goods Inventory	=		+		
c.	Ending Finished Goods Inventory	=		−		

Second Quarter:

f.	Gross Margin	=		−		
g.	Operating Expenses	=		−		
d.	Cost of Goods Available for Sale	=		+		
e.	Cost of Goods Manufactured	=		−		

Chapter 19, P 5. (Continued)

Third Quarter:

j. _____ Gross Margin = _____ + _____ = _____

k. _____ Sales = _____ + _____ = _____

h. _____ Ending Finished Goods Inventory = _____ − _____ = _____

i. _____ Cost of Goods Manufactured = _____ − _____ = _____

Fourth Quarter:

n. _____ Beginning Finished Goods Inventory = _____ − _____ = _____

m. _____ Net Income = _____ − _____ = _____

l. _____ Cost of Goods Sold = _____ − _____ = _____

Chapter 19, P 6.

1. Analyses showing average actual labor hours worked per board prepared

Hours worked per board = hours worked each week ÷ boards produced each week

Department	WEEK 1		WEEK 2		WEEK 3		WEEK 4	
	First Shift (120 boards)	Second Shift (100 boards)	First Shift (135 boards)	Second Shift (105 boards)	First Shift (140 boards)	Second Shift (115 boards)	First Shift (130 boards)	Second Shift (110 boards)
Molding (hr/board)								
Sanding (hr/board)								
Fiber-Ap (hr/board)								
Finishing (hr/board)								

2. Analyses comparing estimated hours per board to actual hours per board prepared

MOLDING	WEEK 1		WEEK 2		WEEK 3		WEEK 4	
	First Shift (120 boards)	Second Shift (100 boards)	First Shift (135 boards)	Second Shift (105 boards)	First Shift (140 boards)	Second Shift (115 boards)	First Shift (130 boards)	Second Shift (110 boards)
Actual hr/board								
Est. hr/board								
Hours under (over) target								
Percent under (over) target								

SANDING	WEEK 1		WEEK 2		WEEK 3		WEEK 4	
	First Shift (120 boards)	Second Shift (100 boards)	First Shift (135 boards)	Second Shift (105 boards)	First Shift (140 boards)	Second Shift (115 boards)	First Shift (130 boards)	Second Shift (110 boards)
Actual hr/board								
Est. hr/board								
Hours under (over) target								
Percent under (over) target								

Chapter 19, P 6. (Continued)

Department	WEEK 1		WEEK 2		WEEK 3		WEEK 4	
	First Shift	Second Shift	First Shift	Second Shift	First Shift	Second Shift	First Shift	Second Shift
FIBER-AP	(120 boards)	(100 boards)	(135 boards)	(105 boards)	(140 boards)	(115 boards)	(130 boards)	(110 boards)
Actual hr/board								
Est. hr/board								
Hours under (over) target								
Percent under (over) target								

Department	WEEK 1		WEEK 2		WEEK 3		WEEK 4	
	First Shift	Second Shift	First Shift	Second Shift	First Shift	Second Shift	First Shift	Second Shift
FINISHING	(120 boards)	(100 boards)	(135 boards)	(105 boards)	(140 boards)	(115 boards)	(130 boards)	(110 boards)
Actual hr/board								
Est. hr/board								
Hours under (over) target								
Percent under (over) target								

Chapter 19, P 7.

1. Types of needed information identified

2. The four *W*s considered

   a. Why prepare the report?

   b. What information should the report contain to meet its purpose?

   c. For whom is the report being prepared? To whom should the report be distributed? Who will read the report?

   d. When is the report due?

Chapter 19, P 7. (Continued)

3. Report format designed

Goodfit Industries, Inc.
Shirts by Olene Sales Analysis
For the Years 20x1, 20x2, 20x3

Sales Representative	20x1 Sales	20x1 Percent of Total Sales	20x1 Percent Growth	20x2 Sales	20x2 Percent of Total Sales	20x2 Percent Growth	20x3 Sales	20x3 Percent of Total Sales	20x3 Percent Growth
1.									
2.									
3.									
4.									
5.									
6.									
7.									
8.									
9.									
10.									

Chapter 19, P 8.

1. Accounts in manufacturing and merchandising organizations identified

a.

b.

2. Key figures calculated

a.	Gross Margin	=		+	
		=		+	
		=			

b.	Cost of Goods Sold	=		−	
		=		−	
		=			

c.	Cost of Goods Available for Sale	=		+	
		=		+	
		=			

d.	Cost of Goods Manufactured	=		−	
		=		−	
		=			

Chapter 19, SD 5.

1.a. The differences in pounds and in percentages are as follows:

	Scrap in Pounds		Difference	
	Actual	Expected	Pounds	Percentage
Machine 1				
Week 1				
Week 2				
Week 3				
Week 4				
Machine 2				
Week 1				
Week 2				
Week 3				
Week 4				

Chapter 19, SD 5. (Continued)

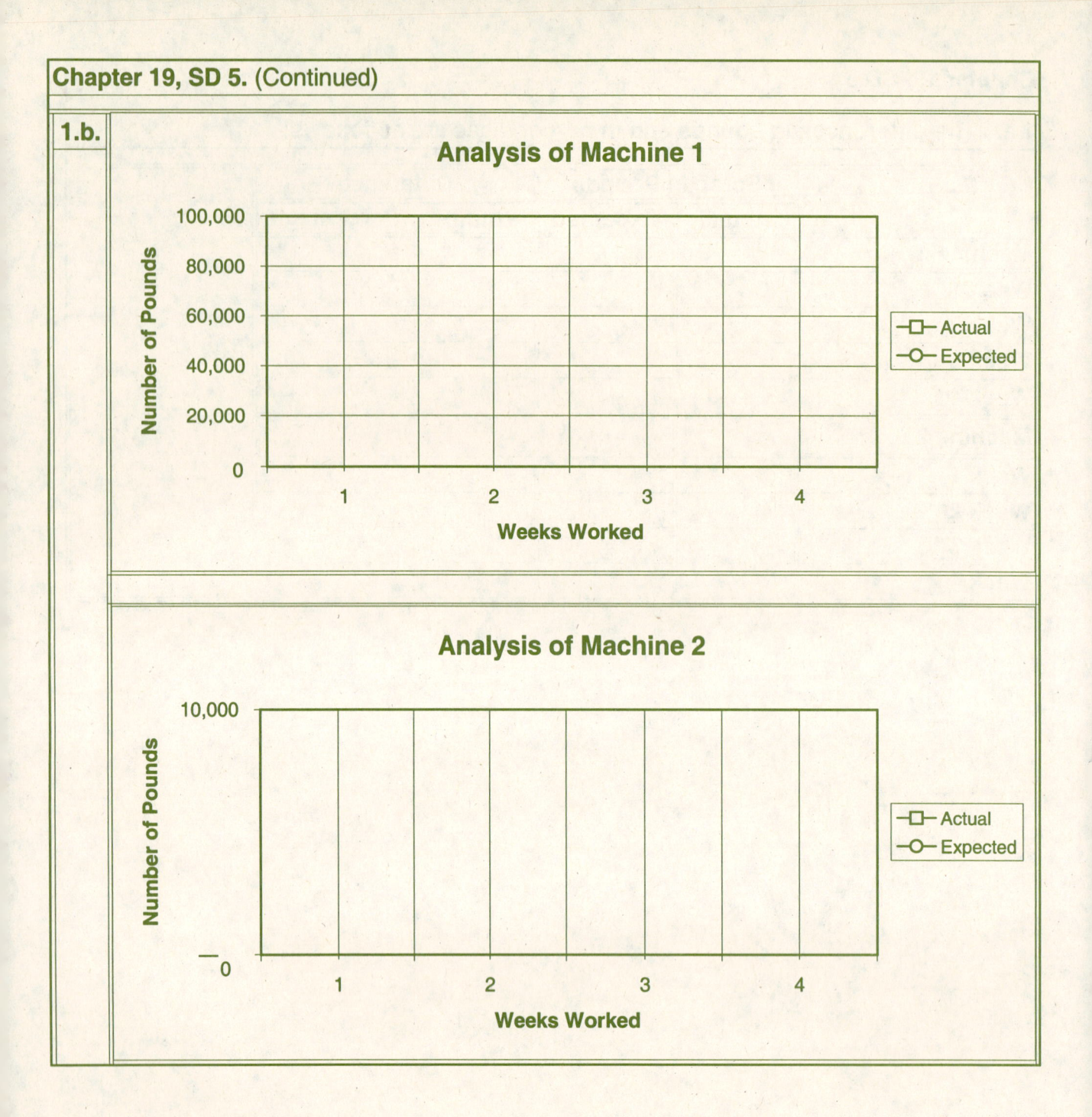

1.b.

Analysis of Machine 1

Analysis of Machine 2

Chapter 19, MRA 4.

1. Average labor hours worked per board calculated

WEEK 1

	First Shift Actual Hours	Average Hours per Board (120 boards)	Second Shift Actual Hours	Average Hours per Board (100 boards)
Molding				
Sanding				
Fiber-Ap				
Finishing				

WEEK 2

	First Shift Actual Hours	Average Hours per Board (135 boards)	Second Shift Actual Hours	Average Hours per Board (105 boards)
Molding				
Sanding				
Fiber-Ap				
Finishing				

WEEK 3

	First Shift Actual Hours	Average Hours per Board (140 boards)	Second Shift Actual Hours	Average Hours per Board (115 boards)
Molding				
Sanding				
Fiber-Ap				
Finishing				

WEEK 4

	First Shift Actual Hours	Average Hours per Board (130 boards)	Second Shift Actual Hours	Average Hours per Board (110 boards)
Molding				
Sanding				
Fiber-Ap				
Finishing				

Chapter 19, MRA 4. (Continued)

2. **Comparative line graphs prepared**

	Molding Department			
	Week 1	**Week 2**	**Week 3**	**Week 4**
First shift				
Second shift				
Estimated				

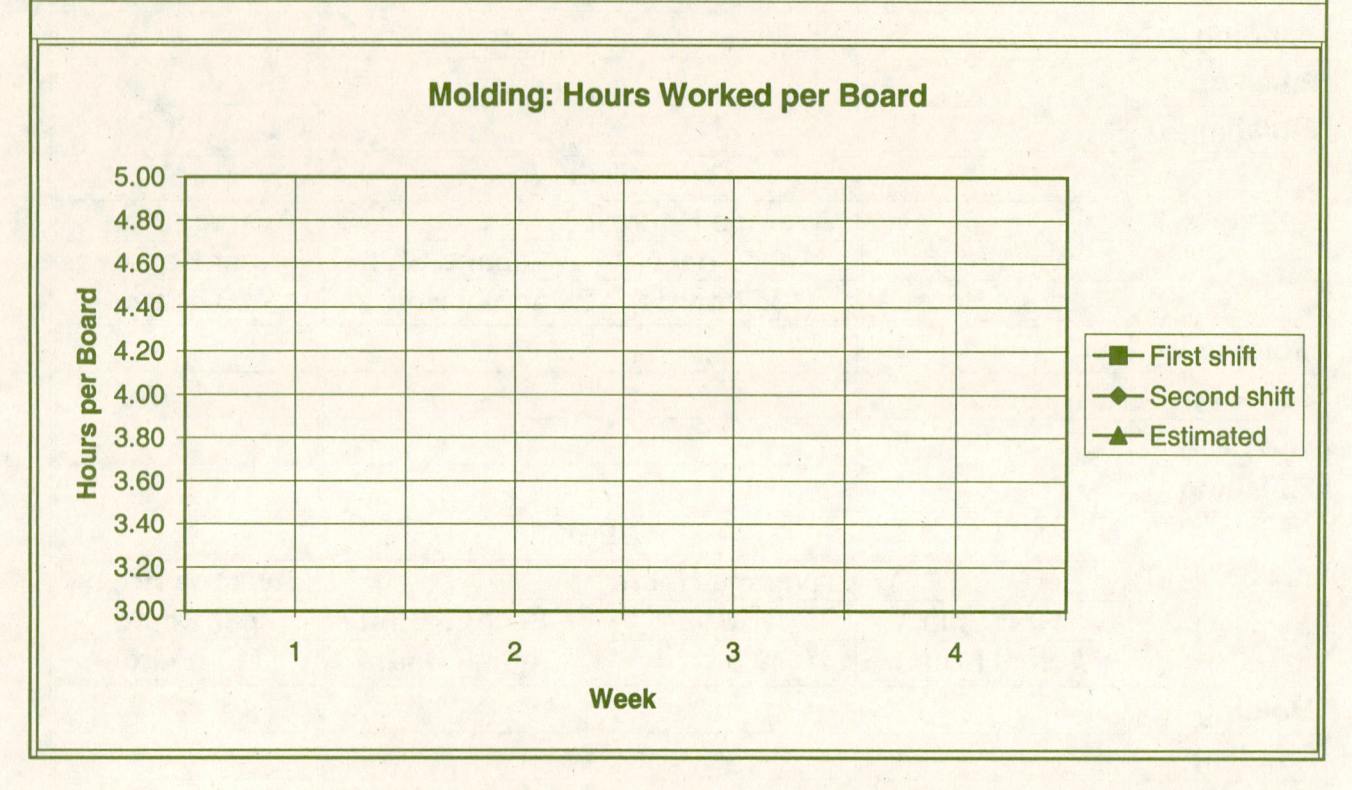

Molding: Hours Worked per Board

Chapter 19, MRA 4. (Continued)

2. (Continued)

	Sanding Department			
	Week 1	Week 2	Week 3	Week 4
First shift				
Second shift				
Estimated				

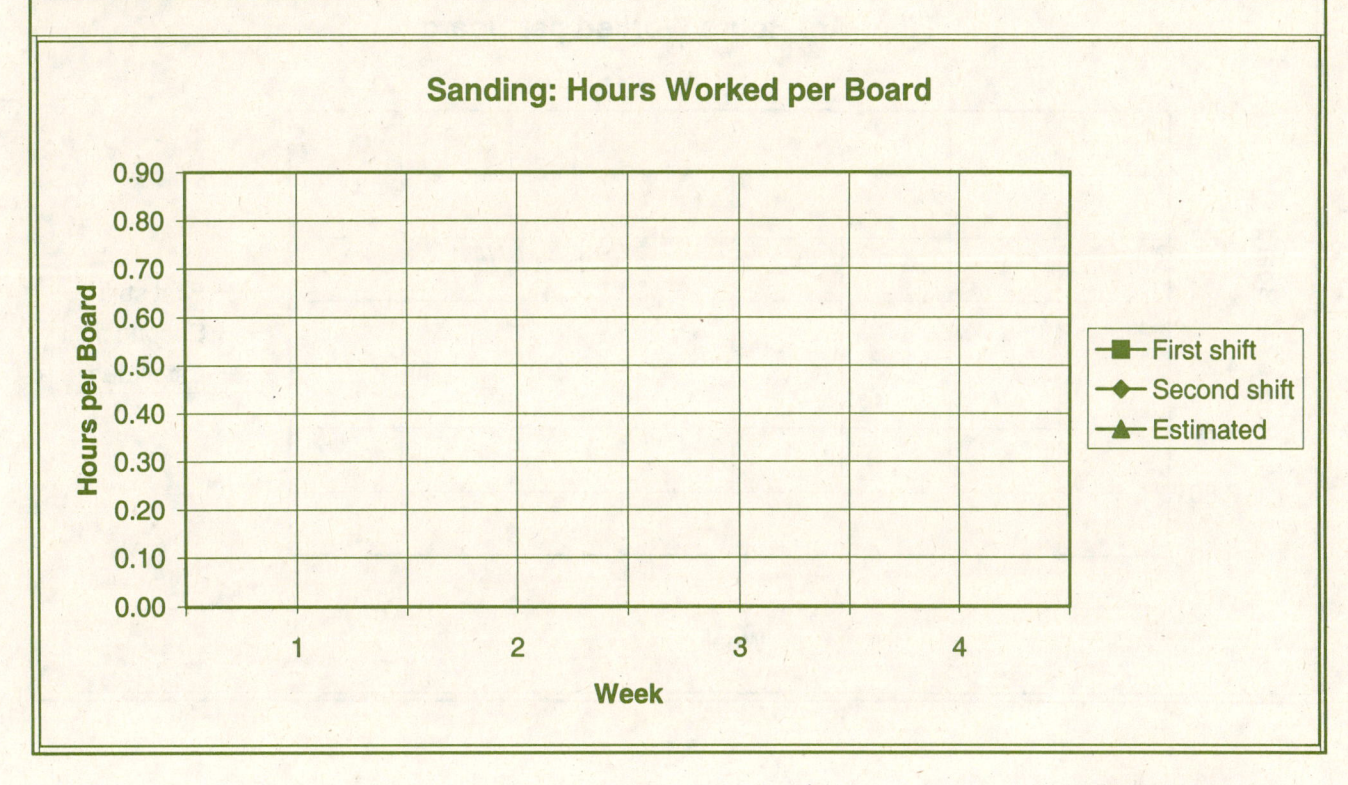

Sanding: Hours Worked per Board

Chapter 19, MRA 4. (Continued)

	Fiber-Ap Department			
	Week 1	**Week 2**	**Week 3**	**Week 4**
First shift				
Second shift				
Estimated				

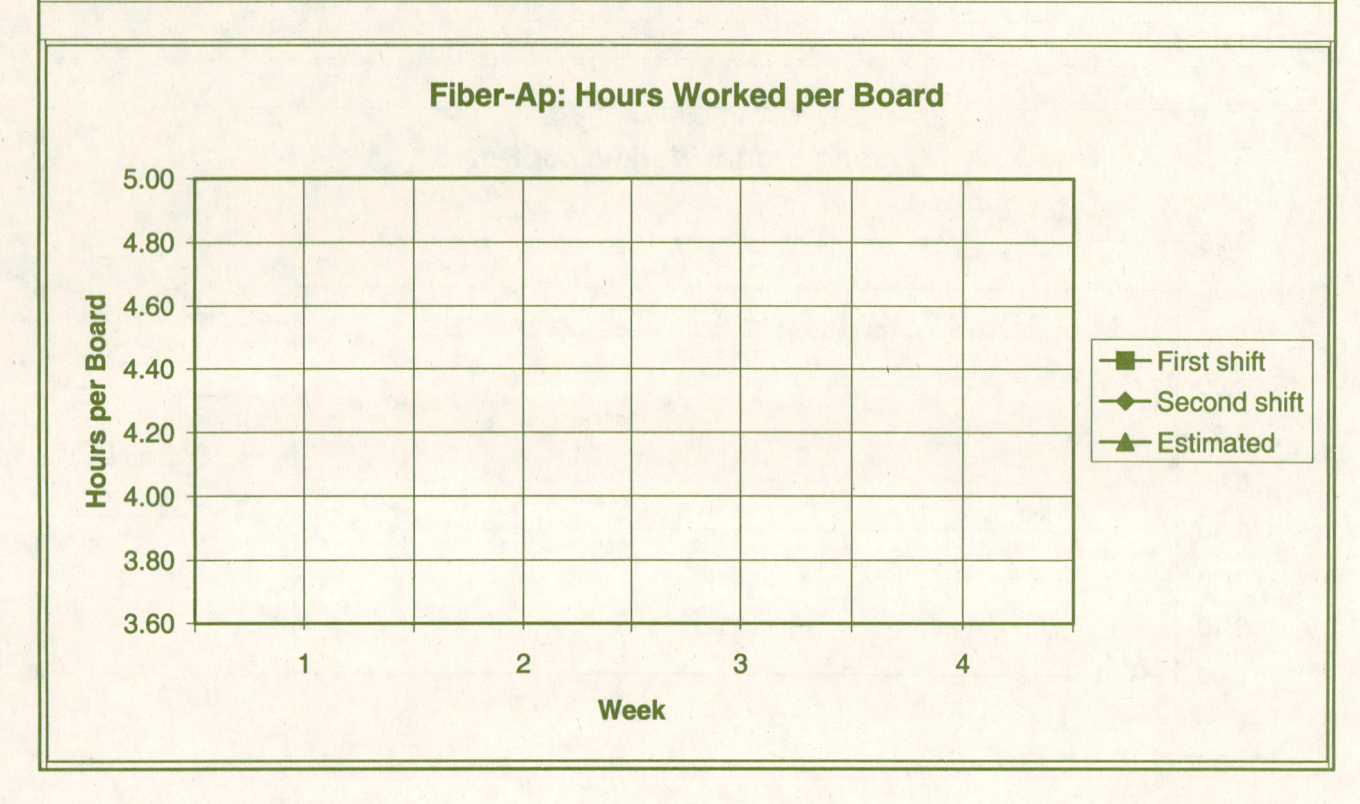

Fiber-Ap: Hours Worked per Board

Chapter 19, MRA 4. (Continued)

2. (Continued)

	Finishing Department			
	Week 1	**Week 2**	**Week 3**	**Week 4**
First shift				
Second shift				
Estimated				

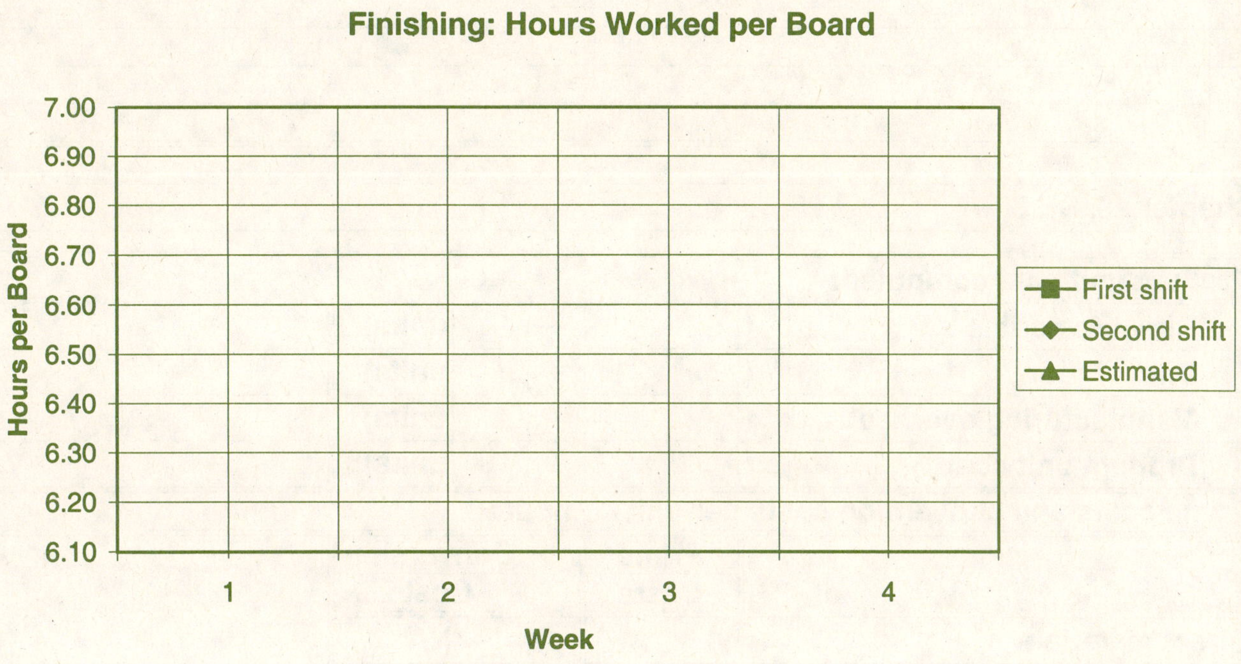

Finishing: Hours Worked per Board
7.00
6.90
6.80
6.70
6.60
6.50
6.40
6.30
6.20
6.10
Hours per Board
1
2
3
4
Week
First shift
Second shift
Estimated

3. Efficiency of shifts discussed

Chapter 20, SE 1.

1.
2.
3.

Chapter 20, SE 2.

1.
2.
3.
4.
5.
6.
7.

Chapter 20, SE 3.

Product unit cost computed:

Direct materials	(		÷	units)	
Direct labor	(		÷	units)	
Manufacturing overhead	(		÷	units)	
Product unit cost	(		÷	units)	

Prime costs and conversion costs per unit computed:

	Prime Costs	Conversion Costs	
Direct materials		NA	
Direct labor			
Manufacturing overhead	NA		
Totals			

Chapter 20, SE 4.

Materials Inventory, ending balance:

Materials Inventory, beginning balance	
Direct materials purchased	
Direct materials placed into production	
Materials Inventory, ending balance	

Work in Process Inventory, ending balance:

Work in Process Inventory, beginning balance	
Direct materials placed into production	
Direct labor costs	
Manufacturing overhead costs	
Cost of goods completed	
Work in Process Inventory, ending balance	

Finished Goods Inventory, ending balance:

Finished Goods Inventory, beginning balance	
Cost of goods completed	
Cost of goods sold	
Finished Goods Inventory, ending balance	

Chapter 20, SE 5.

1.
2.
3.
4.
5.
6.
7.

Chapter 20, SE 6.

C.L.I.N.T. Company
Income Statement
For the Year Ended December 31, 20x2

Sales		
Cost of Goods Sold		
Finished Goods Inventory, December 31, 20x1		
Cost of Goods Manufactured		
Total Cost of Goods Available for Sale		
Less Finished Goods Inventory,		
December 31, 20x2		
Cost of Goods Sold		
Gross Margin		
Operating Expenses		
Income from Operations		
Interest Expense		
Net Income		

Chapter 20, SE 7.

Applied manufacturing overhead	
Less actual manufacturing overhead	
Overapplied	

Chapter 20, SE 8.

Predetermined Overhead Rate per Service Request	=	
	=	service requests
	=	

Chapter 20, SE 9.

Manufacturing Overhead Costs Applied	=		per direct labor hour
		x	direct labor hours
	=		

Chapter 20, SE 10.

Cutting/Stitching

	÷		machine hours	=		per machine hour

Trimming/Packing

	÷		operator hours	=		per operator hour

Designing

	÷		designer hours	=		per designer hour

Chapter 20, SE 11.

Total cost to pick onions:		+ (		x		) =	
Cost per acre to pick onions:		÷		acres =			

Chapter 20, E 1.

1.
2.
3.
4.

Chapter 20, E 2.

	Cost Classification			
	Direct or Indirect	Variable or Fixed	Value-adding or Nonvalue-adding	Product or Period
Example: Bicycle tire				
1. Depreciation on office computer				
2. Labor to assemble bicycle				
3. Labor to inspect bicycle				
4. President's salary				
5. Lubricant for wheels				

Note: Depreciation on office computer and president's salary are not product costs. Therefore, they would not be traceable to the bicycles in a traditional business operation. The two costs would be shown on the income statement as selling and administrative expenses.

Chapter 20, E 3.

1. Unit cost computed

Cost Items	Total Cost	Unit Cost (Total ÷)
Total direct materials costs		
Total direct labor costs		
Total manufacturing overhead cost		
Total production costs		

2. Recommendation made

Chapter 20, E 3. (Continued)

3. **Prime costs and conversion costs per unit computed**

	Prime Costs	Conversion Costs
Direct materials		NA
Direct labor		
Manufacturing overhead	NA	
Totals		

Chapter 20, E 4.

Memo

To:
From:
Topic:

The purpose of each document is:

Purchase Request

Purchase Order

Receiving Report

Materials Request

If you have any additional questions or concerns, I would be happy to discuss them with you.

Sincerely,

Rena Paul

Chapter 20, E 5.

1.
2.
3.
4.
5.
6.
7.

Chapter 20, E 6.

Banty Company
Statement of Cost of Goods Manufactured
For the Month Ended August 31, 20x3

Direct Materials Used		
Materials Inventory, July 31, 20x3		
Direct Materials Purchased		
Cost of Direct Materials Available for Use		
Less Materials Inventory, August 31, 20x3		
Cost of Direct Materials Used		
Direct Labor (hours x)		
Manufacturing Overhead		
Utilities		
Supervision		
Indirect Materials		
Depreciation		
Insurance		
Miscellaneous		
Total Manufacturing Overhead		
Total Manufacturing Costs		
Add Work in Process Inventory, July 31, 20x3		
Total Cost of Work in Process During the Month		
Less Work in Process Inventory, August 31, 20x3		
Cost of Goods Manufactured		

Chapter 20, E 7.

1 and 2. 20x1 and 20x2 predetermined overhead rates computed

	(1) 20x1	(2) 20x2 Percentage	(3) 20x2 (1 × 2)
Indirect materials and supplies			
Repairs and maintenance			
Outside service contracts			
Indirect labor			
Factory supervision			
Depreciation, machinery			
Factory insurance			
Property taxes			
Heat, light, and power			
Miscellaneous manufacturing overhead			
Totals			
Divided by machine hours			*
Predetermined overhead rates	/MH		/MH
*(+ = —)			

Chapter 20, E 8.

1. Anticipated manufacturing overhead determined

| | x | | = | |

2. Manufacturing overhead rate computed

Increase in labor hours:

| | hours | x | | = | | hours |

Predetermined overhead rate:

| | ÷ | | hours | = | | * per labor hour |

3. Manufacturing overhead applied

| | x | | hours | = | | * |

Chapter 20, E 9.

1. Overhead applied to operations computed

| | hours | x | | per hour | = | |

2. Overapplied overhead computed

Overhead applied	
Less overhead incurred	
Overapplied overhead	

3. Effect of overapplied overhead on Cost of Goods Sold determined

| |
| |
| |
| |

*Rounded.

Chapter 20, E 10.

Traditional costing method

x	=		

Activity-based costing method

Activity	Activity Cost Rate		Order HL14 Activity Usage	
Income materials inspection	per type of material	x	types of materials	=
In-process inspection	per product	x	products	=
Tool and gauge control	per process	x	processes	=
Product certification	per order	x	order	=
Total quality control costs assigned to Order HL14				

Chapter 20, E 11.

Gas						
Tractor maintenance						
Tractor depreciation		(		÷	months)	
Labor						
Total costs						
Cost per bale	=		÷		bales	=
Revenue per bale	=		÷		bales	=

Chapter 20, P 1.

1 and 2. Unit cost by department and total unit cost computed

Department 60:

Direct materials used				
	÷		discs	
Direct labor				
	÷		discs	
Manufacturing overhead				
	÷		discs	
Total unit cost, Dept. 60				

Department 61:

Direct materials used				
	÷		discs	
Direct labor				
	÷		discs	
Manufacturing overhead				
	÷		discs	
Total unit cost, Dept. 61				

Total unit cost

3. Analysis of the Gael Company order

Selling price	
Unit cost	
Gross margin per unit	
Gross margin as a percentage of sales:	, or

Chapter 20, P 1. (Continued)

4. Prime costs and conversion costs per unit computed

	Department 60		Department 61	
	Prime Costs	Conversion Costs	Prime Costs	Conversion Costs
Direct materials		NA		NA
Direct labor				
Manufacturing overhead				
Totals				

Chapter 20, P 2.

Plano Vineyards
Statement of Cost of Goods Manufactured
For the Year Ended October 31, 20x1

Direct Materials Used		
Materials Inventory, October 31, 20x0		
Direct Materials Purchased (net)		
Cost of Direct Materials Available for Use		
Less Materials Inventory, October 31, 20x1		
Cost of Direct Materials Used		
Direct Labor		
Manufacturing Overhead		
Depreciation, Plant and Equipment		
Indirect Labor		
Property Tax, Plant and Equipment		
Plant Maintenance		
Small Tools		
Utilities		
Employee Benefits		
Total Manufacturing Overhead		
Total Manufacturing Costs		
Add Work in Process Inventory, October 31, 20x0		
Total Cost of Work in Process During the Year		
Less Work in Process Inventory, October 31, 20x1		
Cost of Goods Manufactured		

Chapter 20, P 3.

	Lillor Division	Berne Division	Lubbock Division	Secco Division
Direct materials used			(g)	
Direct labor	(a)			
Manufacturing overhead				(j)
Total manufacturing costs		(d)	(h)	
Beginning Work in Process Inventory		(e)		(l)
Ending Work in Process Inventory	(b)			
Cost of goods manufactured				(k)
Beginning Finished Goods Inventory		(f)		
Ending Finished Goods Inventory			(i)	
Cost of goods sold	(c)			

Chapter 20, P 4.

1. Predetermined overhead rate computed

Dai Products, Inc.
Overhead Rate Computation Schedule
For the Year Ended December 31, 20x3

Overhead Cost Item	(1) 20x1	(2) 20x2	(3) Projected Percentage Increase	(4) Projection for 20x3 (2 × 3)
Indirect materials				
Indirect labor				
Supervision				
Utilities				
Labor-related costs				
Depreciation, factory				
Depreciation, machinery				
Property taxes				
Insurance				
Miscellaneous manufacturing overhead				
Total manufacturing overhead				

Predetermined overhead rate for the year 20x3:

| | ÷ | | machine hours | | * per machine hour |

*Rounded.

Chapter 20, P 4. (Continued)

2. Amount of applied overhead determined

Job No.	Actual Machine Hours	x	Rate	Overhead Applied*
H–142				
H–164				
H–175				
H–201				
H–218				
H–304				
Totals				

*Rounded.

3. Computation and adjustment of underapplied overhead

Actual overhead incurred in 20x3		
Manufacturing overhead applied		
Underapplied overhead		
Cost of Goods Sold by		.

Chapter 20, P 5.

1 and 2. Total costs assigned to the Altun order

		Traditional Costing Method	Activity-Based Costing Method
Cost of direct materials			
Cost of purchased parts			
Direct labor costs			
x	hours		
Manufacturing overhead cost:			
Traditional costing method			
x			
Activity-based costing method			
Engineering systems design			
	per engineering hour		
x	engineering hours		
Setup			
	per setup		
x	setups		
Parts production			
	per machine hour		
x	machine hours		
Assembly			
	per assembly hour		
x	assembly hours		
Packaging			
	per packaging hour		
x	packaging hours		
Building-occupancy-related overhead			
x	machine hours		
Total costs assigned to the Altun order			

Chapter 20, P 5. (Continued)

3. Cost differences discussed

Chapter 20, P 6.

1. Predetermined overhead rate computed

Features Cosmetics Company
Overhead Rate Computation Schedule
For the Year Ended December 31, 20x2

Overhead Cost Item	(1) 20x0	(2) 20x1	(3) Projected Percentage Increase	(4) Projection 20x2 (2 × 3)
Indirect labor				
Employee benefits				
Manufacturing supervision				
Utilities				
Factory insurance				
Janitorial services				
Depreciation, factory and machinery				
Miscellaneous manufacturing overhead				*
Total manufacturing overhead				

Predetermined overhead rate for 20x2:

_____ ÷ _____ machine hours = _____ per machine hour

*Rounded.

Chapter 20, P 6. (Continued)

2. Amount of applied overhead determined

Job No.	Machine Hours	Predetermined Overhead Rate	Overhead Applied*
2214			**
2215			**
2216			**
2217			**
2218			**
2219			**
Totals			**

*Machine hours   x
**Rounded.

3. Computation and adjustment of overapplied overhead

Manufacturing overhead applied		
Actual overhead incurred in 20x2		
Overapplied overhead		
	Cost of Goods Sold by	.

Chapter 20, P 7.

1 and 2. Total costs assigned to the Winkowsky order

		Traditional Costing Method	Activity-Based Costing Method
Direct materials cost			
Cost of purchased parts			
Direct labor cost			
x	DLH		
Manufacturing overhead cost:			
Traditional costing method			
x			
Activity-based costing method			
Electrical engineering design			
	per engineering hour		
x	engineering hours		
Setup			
	per setup		
x	setups		
Parts production			
	per machine hour		
x	machine hours		
Product testing			
	per product testing hour		
x	product testing hours		
Packaging			
	per packaging hour		
x	packaging hours		
Building-occupancy-related overhead			
x	machine hours		
Total costs assigned to the Winkowsky order			

Chapter 20, P 7. (Continued)

3. Cost difference discussed

Chapter 20, P 8.

1. Calculations using activity-based costing

a. Activity cost rates calculated

Activity Pool	(1) Estimated Activity Pool Amount	(2) Total Estimated Cost Driver Level	(3) Activity Cost Rate (1 ÷ 2)
Setup		setups	per setup
Inspection		inspections	per inspection
Engineering		engineering hours	per engineering hour
Assembly		machine hours	per machine hour
Total			

Chapter 20, P 8. (Continued)

b. Overhead costs applied

Activity Pool	Activity Cost Rate	Rigger II			BioScout		
		Cost Driver Level		Cost Applied	Cost Driver Level		Cost Applied
Setup	per setup		setups	×		setups	×
Inspection	per inspection		inspections	×		inspections	×
Engineering	per engineering hour		engineering hours	×		engineering hours	×
Assembly	per machine hour		machine hours	×		machine hours	×
Total overhead costs applied							
Number of units				÷			÷
Overhead cost per unit							

c. Product unit cost calculated

Product costs per unit:	Rigger II	BioScout
Direct materials		
Direct labor		
Manufacturing overhead		
Product unit cost		

Chapter 20, P 8. (Continued)

2. Differences in assigned costs discussed

	Rigger II	BioScout
Product unit cost:		
Traditional		
ABC		
Difference: decrease (increase)		

Chapter 20, SD 5.

1. Cost per patient day computed

Equipment usage					
Doctors' care	(	x	)		
Special nursing care	(	x	)		
Regular nursing care	(	x	)		
Medications					
Medical supplies					
Room rental					
Food and services					
Total cost per patient day					

2 and 3. Billing per patient day computed

	Cost	2. Normal Billing		3. Industry Average Billing Approach	
Equipment usage		x	*	x	*
Doctors' care		x		x	
Special nursing care		x		x	
Regular nursing care		x	*	x	
Medications		x	*	x	*
Medical supplies		x	*	x	
Room rental		x		x	
Food and services		x		x	
Totals					

*Rounded.

4. Billing procedure recommended

Chapter 20, MRA 1.

1. Ratios computed

a. Ratios of cost of direct materials used, direct labor, and total manufacturing overhead to total manufacturing costs

	20x1		20x0	
	Amount	Ratio	Amount	Ratio
Cost of direct materials used				*
Direct labor				
Total manufacturing overhead				
Total manufacturing costs				

*Adjusted for total of percentages to equal 100.0%.

b. Ratios of sales salaries and commission expense, advertising expense, other selling expenses, administrative expenses, and total selling and administrative expenses to sales.

	20x1		20x0	
	Amount	Ratio	Amount	Ratio
Sales salaries and commission expense				
Advertising expense				
Other selling expenses				
Administrative expenses				
Total selling and administrative expenses				
Sales				

c. Ratios of gross margin, total selling and administrative expenses, and net income to sales

	20x1		20x0	
	Amount	Ratio	Amount	Ratio
Gross margin				
Net income				
Sales				

Chapter 20, MRA 1. (Continued)

2. Comments on ratios

   a.

   b.

   c.

3. Other factors and ratios suggested

Chapter 20, MRA 3.

1. Statement of cost of goods manufactured and income statement prepared

Muntok Pharmaceuticals Corporation
Statement of Cost of Goods Manufactured
For the Month Ended April 30, 20x1

Cost of Direct Materials Used*		
Direct Labor		
Manufacturing Overhead		
Total Manufacturing Costs		
Add Work in Process Inventory, March 31, 20x1		
Total Cost of Work in Process During the Month		
Less Work in Process Inventory, April 30, 20x1		
Cost of Goods Manufactured		
*Cost of Direct Materials Used = + −		

Muntok Pharmaceuticals Corporation
Income Statement
For the Month Ended April 30, 20x1

Sales		
Cost of Goods Sold		
Finished Goods Inventory, March 31, 20x1		
Cost of Goods Manufactured		
Total Cost of Finished Goods Available for Sale		
Less Finished Goods Inventory, April 30, 20x1		
Cost of Goods Sold		
Gross Margin		
Operating Expenses		
General and Administrative Expenses		
Net Income		

Chapter 20, MRA 3. (Continued)

2.

3. If you want to know the profitability of a product line, then you must obtain the following information for *that* line:
   a. Direct materials:
   b. Direct labor:
   c. Overhead costs associated specifically with the production of each product line
   d. Other costs that may be directly traceable to the product:

4. a.
   b.
   c.
   d.
   e.

Chapter 20, MRA 4.

1. **Calculations using the traditional method**

   a. Predetermined overhead rate computed

   Overhead rate = _____ ÷ _____ direct labor hours = _____ per direct labor hour

   b. Total overhead cost applied to each product line computed

	Rigger II			BioScout		
	Cost Driver Level		Cost Applied	Cost Driver Level		Cost Applied
		× DLH			× DLH	

   Overhead costs applied:
   Total manufacturing overhead:
      $25 per DLH
      ÷ Number of units
   Manufacturing overhead cost
      per unit

   c. Product unit cost calculated

	Rigger II	BioScout
Product costs per unit:		
Direct materials		
Direct labor		
Manufacturing overhead		
Product unit cost		

Chapter 20, MRA 4. (Continued)

2. Calculations using activity-based costing

    a. Activity cost rates calculated

Activity Pool	Estimated Activity Pool Amount	Total Estimated Cost Driver Level		Activity Cost Rate	
Setup			setups		per setup
Inspection			inspections		per inspection
Engineering			engineering hours		per engineering hour
Assembly			machine hours		per machine hour
Total					

Chapter 20, MRA 4. (Continued)

b. Overhead costs applied

			Rigger II			BioScout	
Activity Pool	Activity Cost Rate		Cost Driver Level		Cost Applied	Cost Driver Level		Cost Applied
Setup	per setup	×	setups			setups	×	
Inspection	per inspection	×	inspections			inspections	×	
Engineering	per engineering hour	×	engineering hours			engineering hours	×	
Assembly	per machine hour	×	machine hours			machine hours	×	
Total overhead costs applied							
Number of units				÷			÷
Overhead cost per unit							

807

Chapter 20, MRA 4. (Continued)

c. Product costs per unit calculated

	Rigger II	BioScout
Product costs per unit:		
Direct materials		
Direct labor		
Manufacturing overhead		
Product unit cost		

3. Differences in assigned costs discussed

	Rigger II	BioScout
Product costs per unit:		
Traditional		
ABC		
Difference: decrease (increase)		

Chapter 21, SE 1.

1.
2.
3.

Chapter 21, SE 2.

1.		4.	
2.		5.	
3.		6.	

Chapter 21, SE 3.

Work in Process Inventory		Manufacturing Overhead	
(1)		(1)	(2)
(2)			

Marketing Expense		Factory Payroll	
(1)			(1)

Chapter 21, SE 4.

1.
2.
3.
4.
5.
6.

Chapter 21, SE 5.

		Job Order	168
Job Order Cost Card			
Gatekeeper 3000			
Apache City, North Dakota			
Customer Robert Arthur	**Batch**	**Custom**	X
Specifications 6 custom computer systems			
Date of Order 4/4/x3	**Date of Completion**	6/8/x3	

Costs Charged to Job	Previous Months	Current Month	Cost Summary
Direct materials			
Direct labor			
Manufacturing overhead applied			
Totals			
Units completed			6
Product unit cost			

Chapter 21, SE 6.

Blue Blaze
Schedule of Equivalent Production
For the Month Ended July 31, 20x7

Units—Stage of Completion	Units to Be Accounted For	Equivalent Units Direct Materials Costs	Equivalent Units Conversion Costs
Beginning inventory—units started last period but completed in this period			
Units started and completed in this period (–)			
Ending inventory—units started but not completed in this period			
Direct materials costs—100% complete			
Conversion costs—70% complete (70% x)			
Totals			

Chapter 21, SE 7.

Blue Blaze
Schedule of Equivalent Production
For the Month Ended July 31, 20x7

Units—Stage of Completion	Units to Be Accounted For	Equivalent Units Direct Materials Costs	Equivalent Units Conversion Costs
Beginning inventory—units started last period but completed in this period			
Direct materials costs—100% complete			
Conversion costs—40% complete (60% x)			
Units started and completed in this period (–)			
Ending inventory—units started but not completed in this period			
Direct materials costs—100% complete			
Conversion costs—70% complete (70% x)			
Totals			

Chapter 21, SE 8.

Blue Blaze
Unit Cost Analysis Schedule
For the Month Ended July 31, 20x7

Total Cost Analysis	Costs from Beginning Inventory	Current Period Costs	Total Costs to Be Accounted For
Direct materials costs			
Conversion costs			
Totals			

Computation of Equivalent Unit Costs	Current Period Costs	÷ Equivalent Units	= Cost per Equivalent Unit
Direct materials costs			
Conversion costs			
Totals			

Chapter 21, SE 9.

Blue Blaze
Cost Summary Schedule
For the Month Ended July 31, 20x7

	Cost of Goods Transferred to Finished Goods Inventory	Cost of Ending Work in Process Inventory	Total Costs to Be Accounted For
Beginning inventory			
Costs from preceding period			
Costs to complete this period			
Units started and completed			
units x per unit			
Ending inventory			
Direct materials costs:			
units x			
Conversion costs:			
units x			
Totals			

Chapter 21, SE 10.

Chapter 21, E 1.

1.		6.	
2.		7.	
3.		8.	
4.		9.	
5.		10.	

Chapter 21, E 2.

a.	
b.	
c.	
d.	
e.	
f.	
g.	
h.	

* Either method could be used, depending on specifications.

Chapter 21, E 3.

a.	
b.	
c.	
d.	
e.	
f.	
g.	
h.	

Chapter 21, E 4.

1. T accounts prepared

Materials Inventory		Work in Process Inventory	
(c)	(a)	Beg. Bal. 29,400	
	(c)	(a)	
		(b)	
		(d)	

Manufacturing Overhead		Factory Payroll	
(b)	(d)*		(b)
(c)			

		Accounts Payable	
			(c)

* _____ × _____ = _____

2. Ending balance computed

Work in Process Inventory account:	
Beginning balance, June 30	
Debits during July:	
Direct materials	
Direct labor	
Manufacturing overhead	
Less transfers to Finished Goods Inventory	
Ending balance, July 31	

Chapter 21, E 5.

Job Order Cost Card
Hoptung Cabinet Company

Job Order: A-62

| Customer | Sally's Cabinets, Inc. | Batch | | Custom | X |

Specifications: Kitchen cabinets per customer

Date of Order: 1/10/xx Date of Completion: 1/24/xx

Costs Charged to Job	Previous Months	Current Month	Cost Summary
Direct Materials			
Cedar			
Pine			
Hardware			
Assembly supplies			
Total direct materials			
Direct Labor			
Sawing			
Shaping			
Finishing			
Assembly			
Total direct labor			
Manufacturing Overhead			
(per machine hour)			
Sawing (hours)			
Shaping (hours)			
Finishing (hours)			
Assembly (hours)			
Total manufacturing overhead			
Total Cost			
Units completed			
Product unit cost			

Chapter 21, E 6.

Total manufacturing costs:

	Liability insurance, manufacturing	
	Depreciation, manufacturing equipment	
	Direct materials	
	Indirect labor, manufacturing	
	Indirect materials	
	Heat, light, and power, manufacturing	
	Fire insurance, manufacturing	
	Rent, manufacturing	
	Direct labor	
	Manager's salary, manufacturing	
	Total manufacturing costs	

Computation of product unit cost:

	÷	units =	* per unit

*Rounded.

Chapter 21, E 7.

1. **Total cost of each job computed**

Nanette Corporation
Special Cost Analysis
August

	Job Order Cost Cards		
	Job A–25	Job A–27	Job B–14
Direct materials:			
Fabric Q			
Fabric Z			
Fabric YB			
Total			
Direct labor:			
Garmentmaker			
Layout			
Packaging			
Total			
Manufacturing overhead:			
120% of direct labor cost			
Total cost			

2. **Product unit cost for each job computed**

Units produced			
Product unit cost	*	*	*

*Rounded.

Chapter 21, E 8.

JOB ORDER COST CARD
Harold Computer Services

Customer:	Ray Dove
Job Order No.:	
Contract Type:	Cost-Plus
Type of Service:	Software Installation and Internet Interfacing
Date of Completion:	October 6, 20x6

Costs Charged to Job	Total Cost
Software Installation Services	
Installation labor	
Service overhead (50% of installation labor costs)	
Total	
Internet Services	
Internet labor	
Service overhead (of Internet labor costs)	
Total	

Cost Summary to Date	Total Cost
Software Installation Services	
Internet Services	
Total	
Profit margin ( )	
Contract revenue	

Chapter 21, E 9.

Inputs:

Chapter 21, E 10.

Deegan Stone Company
Schedule of Equivalent Production—FIFO Costing Method
For the Year Ended December 31, 20x1

Units—Stage of Completion	Units to Be Accounted For	Equivalent Units Direct Materials Costs	Equivalent Units Conversion Costs
Beginning inventory—units started last period but completed in this period			
Units started and completed in this period			
Ending inventory—units started but not completed in this period (—)			
Direct materials costs—100% complete			
Conversion costs—60% complete (60% x)			
Totals			

Chapter 21, E 11.

Olivares Enterprises
Schedule of Equivalent Production—FIFO Costing Method
For the Month Ended August 31, 20x5

Units—Stage of Completion	Units to Be Accounted For	Equivalent Units Direct Materials Costs	Equivalent Units Conversion Costs
Beginning inventory—units started last period but completed in this period			
Direct materials costs—100% complete			
Conversion costs—80% complete (20% x)			
Units started and completed in this period (—)			
Ending inventory—units started but not completed in this period			
Direct materials costs—100% complete			
Conversion costs—60% complete (x)			
Totals			

Chapter 21, E 12.

Dept.	Direct Materials Costs			Conversion Costs			Total Unit Cost
	Dollars	Equiv. Units	Unit Cost	Dollars	Equiv. Units	Unit Cost	
A							
B							
C							
D							
E							
Totals							

Chapter 21, E 13.

Pittman's Pots, Inc.
Unit Cost Analysis Schedule—FIFO Costing Method
For the Month Ended August 31, 20x2

Total Cost Analysis	Costs from Beginning Inventory	Current Period Costs	Total Costs to Be Accounted For
Direct materials costs			
Conversion costs			
Totals			

Computation of Equivalent Unit Costs	Current Period Costs	÷ Equivalent Units	= Cost per Equivalent Unit
Direct materials costs			
Conversion costs			
Totals			

Chapter 21, E 14.

Upshaw Bakery
Cost Summary Schedule—FIFO Costing Method
For the Month Ended March 31, 20x9

	Cost of Goods Transferred to Finished Goods Inventory	Cost of Ending Work in Process Inventory	Total Costs to Be Accounted For
Beginning inventory			
Beginning balance			
Costs to complete:			
_____ units × 90% × _____ per unit			
Total beginning inventory			
Units started and completed			
_____ units × _____ per unit			
Ending inventory			
Direct materials costs:			
_____ units × _____ per unit			
Conversion costs:			
_____ units × _____ × _____ per unit		*	
Totals			

*Rounded to the nearest dollar.

Chapter 21, E 15.

Chapter 21, P 1.

1. T accounts prepared and unknown values computed

May

Materials Inventory

Beg. Bal.	Requests
(a) Purchases	
End. Bal.	

Work in Process Inventory

Beg. Bal.	(c) Completed
(b) Direct Materials	
Direct Labor	
Mfg. Overhead	
Applied *	
(d) End. Bal.	

Finished Goods Inventory

Beg. Bal.	Sold
(c) Completed	
End. Bal.	

* + =
** × =

June

Materials Inventory

(e) Beg. Bal.	(h) Requests
Purchases	
End. Bal.	

Work in Process Inventory

(f) Beg. Bal.	Completed
(h) Direct Materials	
Direct Labor	
(i) Mfg. Overhead	
Applied **	
(k) End. Bal.	

Finished Goods Inventory

(g) Beg. Bal.	(j) Sold
Completed	
End. Bal.	

Chapter 21, P 2.

1. Entries recorded in T accounts and job order cost cards prepared

Materials Inventory	
9/1	9/3
9/4	9/10
9/23	9/27
End. Bal.	

Work in Process Inventory	
9/3	9/30
9/10	
9/15	
9/15	*
9/27	
9/30	
9/30	**
End. Bal.	

Finished Goods Inventory	
9/30	9/30
End. Bal.	

Manufacturing Overhead	
9/8	9/15
9/10	9/30
9/15	
9/22	
9/27	
9/30	
9/30	
End. Bal.	

Cash	
	9/4
	9/8
	9/22
	End. Bal.

Sales	
	9/30
	End. Bal.

Accounts Receivable	
9/30	
End. Bal.	

Cost of Goods Sold	
9/30	
End. Bal.	

Accumulated Depreciation—Manufacturing Equipment	
	9/30
	End. Bal.

Selling and Administrative Expense	
9/15	
9/30	
End. Bal.	

* _____ x 120% = _____
** _____ x _____ = _____

Chapter 21, P 2. (Continued)

		Accounts Payable		
		9/1		
		9/23		
		End. Bal.		

		Factory Payroll		
		9/15		
		9/30		
		End. Bal.		

		Property Taxes Payable		
		9/30		
		End. Bal.		

Chapter 21, P 2. (Continued)

Job Order Cost Card
Ricardo Industries, Inc.

Job Order: **A**

Customer: **Job A** Batch: _____ Custom: **X**

Specifications: **Uniforms per customer**

Date of Order: **9/3/xx**   Date of Completion: **9/30/xx**

Costs Charged to Job	Previous Months	Current Month	Cost Summary
Direct materials			
Total direct materials			
Direct labor			
Total direct labor			
Manufacturing overhead applied (120% of direct labor costs)			
Total manufacturing overhead			
Total Cost			
Units completed			
Product unit cost			

Chapter 21, P 2. (Continued)

Job Order Cost Card
Ricardo Industries, Inc.

Job Order: B

Customer: Job B Batch: Custom: X
Specifications: Uniforms per customer
Date of Order: 9/27/xx Date of Completion: 9/30/xx

Costs Charged to Job	Previous Months	Current Month	Cost Summary
Direct materials			
Direct labor			
Manufacturing overhead applied (of direct labor costs)			
Total Cost			
Units completed			
Product unit cost			

Job Order Cost Card
Ricardo Industries, Inc.

Job Order: C

Customer: Job C Batch: Custom: X
Specifications: Uniforms per customer
Date of Order: 9/27/xx Date of Completion:

Costs Charged to Job	Previous Months	Current Month	Cost Summary
Direct materials			
Direct labor			
Manufacturing overhead applied (of direct labor costs)			
Total Cost			
Units completed			
Product unit cost			

Chapter 21, P 2. (Continued)

2. Underapplied overhead computed

Manufacturing overhead incurred	
Manufacturing overhead applied	
Underapplied overhead	

Manufacturing Overhead

9/8		9/15	
9/10		9/30	
9/15			
9/22			
9/27			
9/30			
9/30			
		9/30	
End. Bal.			

Cost of Goods Sold

9/30			
9/30			
End. Bal.			

Chapter 21, P 3.

1. Transactions reconstructed using T accounts
4. Ending inventory balances computed

Materials Inventory			
Beg. Bal.		2/4	
2/6		2/13	
2/12		2/25	
2/24			
End. Bal.			

Work in Process Inventory			
Beg. Bal.		2/28	**
2/4			
2/13			
2/14			
2/14			
2/25			
2/28			
2/28			
End. Bal.	***		

Accounts Receivable			
2/28			
End. Bal.			

Finished Goods Inventory			
Beg. Bal.		2/28	*
2/28	**		
End. Bal.			

Manufacturing Overhead			
		2/14	
		2/28	
		End. Bal.	

Factory Payroll			
2/14		2/14	
2/28		2/28	
End. Bal.			

Sales			
		2/28	
		End. Bal.	

Cost of Goods Sold			
2/28	*		
End. Bal.			

* Rounded (　　　÷ 1.70 =　　　)
** 　　　−　　　=　　　
*** Ending Work in Process Inventory:
　　　Job AJ–10
　　　Job AJ–14
　　　Job AJ–30
　　　Job AJ–16
　　　Total

Chapter 21, P 3. (Continued)

2. Cost of completed units computed

Cost of ending Work in Process Inventory:

Job No.	Direct Materials	Direct Labor	Manufacturing Overhead	Total
AJ–10				
AJ–14				
AJ–30				
AJ–16				

Costs of units completed:	
Beginning balance, Work in Process Inventory	
Cost of direct materials, direct labor, and manufacturing overhead added during period	
Total costs included in Work in Process Inventory	
Less ending Work in Process Inventory	
Cost of units completed and transferred	

3. Cost of units sold computed

Sales equal to 170% of cost of units sold

	÷	1.70	=		*

*Rounded to the nearest dollar.

Chapter 21, P 3. (Continued)

5. Product unit costs computed

Job AJ–10:

March beginning balance				
March costs:				
Direct labor				
Manufacturing overhead (140%)				
Total cost				
Product unit cost:		÷ 40 =		

Job AJ–14:

March beginning balance				
March costs:				
Direct labor				
Manufacturing overhead ( )				
Total cost				
Product unit cost:		÷ =	*	

*Rounded.

Chapter 21, P 4.

1. Process cost report with schedule of equivalent production, unit cost analysis schedule, and cost summary schedule prepared

Ossossane Foods, Inc.
Mixing Department
Process Cost Report
For the Month Ended January 31, 20x8

1a. Schedule of equivalent production

Units—Stage of Completion	Units to Be Accounted For	Equivalent Units Direct Materials Costs	Equivalent Units Conversion Costs
Beginning inventory—units started last period but completed in this period			
Direct materials costs—100% complete			
Conversion costs—40% complete			
(60% x)			
Units started and completed in this period			
(–)			
Ending inventory—units started but not completed in this period			
Direct materials costs—100% complete			
Conversion costs—60% complete			
(60% x)			
Totals			

Chapter 21, P 4. (Continued)

1b. Unit cost analysis schedule

Total Cost Analysis	Costs from Beginning Inventory	Current Period Costs	Total Costs to Be Accounted For
Direct materials costs			
Conversion costs			
Totals			

Computation of Equivalent Unit Costs	Current Period Costs	÷	Equivalent Units	=	Cost per Equivalent Unit
Direct materials costs					
Conversion costs					
Totals					

Chapter 21, P 4. (Continued)

1c. Cost summary schedule

	Cost of Goods Transferred to Cooking Department	Cost of Ending Work in Process Inventory	Total Costs to Be Accounted For
Beginning inventory			
Beginning balance			
Cost to complete:			
units x per unit			
Total beginning inventory			
Units started and completed			
units x per unit			
Ending inventory			
Direct materials costs:			
units x per unit			
Conversion costs:			
units x per unit			
Totals			

2. Analysis for the Cooking Department explained

Chapter 21, P 5.

The following unit analysis will help students with this problem's two-part solution.

	July	August
Beginning work in process inventory	2,300	3,050
Plus units started during the month	31,500	32,800
Units to be accounted for	33,800	35,850
Less ending work in process inventory	3,050	3,600
Units completed and transferred	30,750	32,250
Units started during the month	31,500	32,800
Less units in ending work in process inventory	3,050	3,600
Units started and completed	28,450	29,200

Chapter 21, P 5. (Continued)

1. Process cost report with schedule of equivalent production, unit cost analysis schedule, and cost summary schedule prepared

Clean Wash Laboratories
Process Cost Report
For the Month Ended July 31, 20x3

1a. Schedule of equivalent production

Units—Stage of Completion	Units to Be Accounted For	Equivalent Units Direct Materials Costs	Equivalent Units Conversion Costs
Beginning inventory—units started last period but completed in this period			
Direct materials costs—100% complete			
Conversion costs—30% complete			
(x)			
Units started and completed in this period			
Ending inventory—units started but not completed in this period			
Direct materials costs—100% complete			
Conversion costs—60% complete			
(x)			
Totals			

Chapter 21, P 5. (Continued)

1b. Unit cost analysis schedule

Total Cost Analysis	Costs from Beginning Inventory	Current Period Costs	Total Costs to Be Accounted For
Direct materials costs			
Conversion costs			
Totals			

Computation of Equivalent Unit Costs	Current Period Costs	÷	Equivalent Units	=	Cost per Equivalent Unit
Direct materials costs					
Conversion costs					
Totals					

Chapter 21, P 5. (Continued)

1c. Cost summary schedule

	Cost of Goods Transferred to Finished Goods Inventory	Cost of Ending Work in Process Inventory	Total Costs to Be Accounted For
Beginning inventory			
Beginning balance			
Cost to complete:			
_____ units x _____ per unit			
Total beginning inventory			
Units started and completed			
_____ units x _____ per unit			
Ending inventory			
Direct materials costs:			
_____ units x _____ per unit			
Conversion costs:			
_____ units x _____ per unit			
Totals			

2. The amount of _____ should be transferred to the Finished Goods Inventory account.

Chapter 21, P 5. (Continued)

3. Process cost report with schedule of equivalent production, unit cost analysis schedule, and cost summary schedule prepared

Clean Wash Laboratories
Process Cost Report
For the Month Ended August 31, 20x3

3a. Schedule of equivalent production

Units—Stage of Completion	Units to Be Accounted For	Equivalent Units Direct Materials Costs	Equivalent Units Conversion Costs
Beginning inventory—units started last period but completed in this period			
Direct materials costs—100% complete			
Conversion costs—60% complete			
(x)			
Units started and completed in this period			
Ending inventory—units started but not completed in this period			
Direct materials costs—100% complete			
Conversion costs—50% complete			
(x)			
Totals			

Chapter 21, P 5. (Continued)

3b. Unit cost analysis schedule

Total Cost Analysis	Costs from Beginning Inventory	Current Period Costs	Total Costs to Be Accounted For
Direct materials costs			
Conversion costs			
Totals			

Computation of Equivalent Unit Costs	Current Period Costs	÷	Equivalent Units	=	Cost per Equivalent Unit
Direct materials costs					
Conversion costs					
Totals					

Chapter 21, P 5. (Continued)

3c. Cost summary schedule

			Cost of Goods Transferred to Finished Goods Inventory	Cost of Ending Work in Process Inventory	Total Costs to Be Accounted For
Beginning inventory					
Beginning balance					
Cost to complete:					
units	x	per unit			
Total beginning inventory					
Units started and completed					
units	x	per unit			
Ending inventory					
Direct materials costs:					
units	x	per unit			
Conversion costs:					
— units	x	$1.70 per unit			
Totals					

The amount of _____ should be transferred to the Finished Goods Inventory account.

Chapter 21, P 6.

1. Entries recorded in T accounts and job order cost cards prepared

Materials Inventory			
1/1		1/4	
1/2		1/21	
1/19			
End. Bal.			

Work in Process Inventory			
1/4		1/31	
1/15			
1/15			
1/21			
1/31			
1/31			
End. Bal.			

Cash			
		1/10	
		End. Bal.	

Accounts Receivable			
1/31			
End. Bal.			

Prepaid Insurance			
		1/31	
		End. Bal.	

Accumulated Depreciation— Machinery			
		1/31	
		End. Bal.	

Accounts Payable			
		1/1	
		1/2	
		1/19	
		End. Bal.	

Property Taxes Payable			
		1/31	
		End. Bal.	

Finished Goods Inventory			
1/31		1/31	
End. Bal.			

Manufacturing Overhead			
1/4		1/15	
1/10		1/31	
1/15			
1/21			
1/31			
1/31			
End. Bal.			

Sales			
		1/31	
		End. Bal.	

Cost of Goods Sold			
1/31			
End. Bal.			

Selling and Administrative Expense			
1/15			
1/15			
1/31			
1/31			
End. Bal.			

Factory Payroll			
		1/15	
		1/31	
		End. Bal.	

Chapter 21, P 6. (Continued)

		Job Order	X
Job Order Cost Card			
Bogey Carts Manufacturing, Inc.			

Customer	Job X	Batch		Custom	X
Specifications	Golf carts per customer specs					
Date of Order	1/4/xx		Date of Completion	1/31/xx	

Costs Charged to Job	Previous Months	Current Month	Cost Summary
Direct materials			
Total direct materials			
Direct labor			
Total direct labor			
Manufacturing overhead applied			
(of direct labor costs)			
Total manufacturing overhead			
Total Cost			
Units completed			
Product unit cost			

Chapter 21, P 6. (Continued)

Job Order Cost Card
Bogey Carts Manufacturing, Inc.

Job Order: Y

Customer	Job Y	Batch		Custom	X

Specifications: Golf carts per customer specs

Date of Order: 1/21/xx Date of Completion: 1/31/xx

Costs Charged to Job	Previous Months	Current Month	Cost Summary
Direct materials			
Direct labor			
Manufacturing overhead applied (___ of direct labor costs)			
Total Cost			
Units completed			
Product unit cost			

Chapter 21, P 6. (Continued)

		Job Order	Z
Job Order Cost Card			
Bogey Carts Manufacturing, Inc.			
Customer: Job Z	Batch:	Custom:	X
Specifications: Golf carts per customer specs			
Date of Order: 1/21/xx	Date of Completion:		

Costs Charged to Job	Previous Months	Current Month	Cost Summary
Direct materials			
Direct labor			
Manufacturing overhead applied (of direct labor costs)			
Total Cost			
Units completed			
Product unit cost			

Chapter 21, P 6. (Continued)

2. Underapplied overhead computed

Manufacturing overhead incurred	
Manufacturing overhead applied	
Underapplied overhead	

Manufacturing Overhead

1/4		1/15	
1/10		1/31	
1/15			
1/21			
1/31			
1/31			
		1/31	
End. Bal.			

Cost of Goods Sold

1/31			
1/31			
End. Bal.			

Chapter 21, P 7.

1. Transactions reconstructed using T accounts
4. Ending inventory balances computed

Materials Inventory			
Beg. Bal.		6/6	
6/4		6/23	
6/16			
6/22			
End. Bal.			

Finished Goods Inventory			
Beg. Bal.		6/30	*
6/30	**		
End. Bal.			

Work in Process Inventory			
Beg. Bal.		6/30	**
6/6			
6/15			
6/15			
6/23			
6/29			
6/29			
End. Bal.			

Manufacturing Overhead			
		6/15	
		6/29	
		End. Bal.	

Accounts Receivable			
6/30			
End. Bal.			

Factory Payroll			
6/15		6/15	
6/29		6/29	
End. Bal.			

Cost of Goods Sold			
6/30		*	
End. Bal.			

Sales			
		6/30	
		End. Bal.	

* Rounded (÷ 1.75 =   )

**   −   =

Ending Work in Process Inventory:
- Job 24–A
- Job 24–B
- Job 24–C
- Job 24–D
- Total

Chapter 21, P 7. (Continued)

2. Cost of completed units computed

Cost of ending Work in Process Inventory:

Job No.	Direct Materials	Direct Labor	Manufacturing Overhead	Total
24–A				
24–B				
24–C				
24–D				

Costs of units completed:

Beginning balance, Work in Process Inventory	
Cost of direct materials, direct labor, and overhead added during period	
Total costs included in Work in Process Inventory	
Less ending Work in Process Inventory	
Cost of units completed and transferred	

3. Cost of units sold computed

Sales equal to 175% of cost of units sold

	÷		=		*

*Rounded.

Chapter 21, P 7. (Continued)

5. Product unit costs computed

Job 24–A:

July beginning balance					
July costs:					
Direct labor					
Manufacturing overhead (130%)					
Total cost					
Product unit cost:		÷		=	*

Job 24–C:

July beginning balance					
July costs:					
Direct labor					
Manufacturing overhead (130%)					
Total cost					
Product unit cost:		÷		=	*

*Rounded.

Chapter 21, P 8.

1. Process cost report with schedule of equivalent production, unit cost analysis schedule, and cost summary schedule prepared

Lenox Bottling Company
Mixing Department
Process Cost Report
For the Month Ended August 31, 20x2

1a. Schedule of equivalent production

Units—Stage of Completion	Units to Be Accounted For	Equivalent Units — Direct Materials Costs	Equivalent Units — Conversion Costs
Beginning inventory—units started last period but completed in this period			
Direct materials costs—100% complete			
Conversion costs—80% complete			
(x —)			
Units started and completed in this period	*		
Ending inventory—units started but not completed in this period			
Direct materials costs—100% complete			
Conversion costs—50% complete			
(x —)			
Totals			

*   —   or 240,000 − 3,600

Chapter 21, P 8. (Continued)

1b. Unit cost analysis schedule

Total Cost Analysis	Costs from Beginning Inventory	Current Period Costs	Total Costs to Be Accounted For
Direct materials costs			
Conversion costs			
Totals			

Computation of Equivalent Unit Costs	Current Period Costs	÷	Equivalent Units	=	Cost per Equivalent Unit
Direct materials costs					
Conversion costs					
Totals					

Chapter 21, P 8. (Continued)

1c. Cost summary schedule

	Cost of Goods Transferred to Bottling Department	Cost of Ending Work in Process Inventory	Total Costs to Be Accounted For
Beginning inventory			
Beginning balance			
Cost to complete:			
_____ units × _____			
Total beginning inventory			
Units started and completed			
_____ units × _____ per unit			
Ending inventory			
Direct materials costs:			
_____ units × _____ per unit			
Conversion costs:			
_____ units × _____ per unit			
Totals			

2. The amount of _____ should be transferred to the Work in Process Inventory account of the Bottling Department.

Chapter 21, SD 5.

1. **Job order costs and product unit costs computed**

Job Order K–1

		÷		=		per unit

Job Order K–2

Beginning Work in Process Inventory						
Direct materials						
Direct labor						
Overhead (150%)						
Total		÷		=		per unit

Job Order K–4

Direct materials						
Direct labor						
Overhead (150%)						
Total		÷		=		per unit

Job Order K–5

Direct materials		
Direct labor		
Overhead (150%)		
Total		(unfinished)

Chapter 21, SD 5. (Continued)

2. **Job order cost cards prepared and current balances determined**

Job Order: K-2

Job Order Cost Card
Zavala Manufacturing Company

Customer	K-2	Batch		Custom	X

Specifications: Plastic products per customer

Date of Order: x/xx/xx Date of Completion: x/xx/xx

Costs Charged to Job	Previous Months	Current Month	Cost Summary
Direct materials			
Direct labor			
Manufacturing overhead (of direct labor costs)			
Total Cost			
Units completed			
Product unit cost			

Job Order: K-4

Job Order Cost Card
Zavala Manufacturing Company

Customer	K-4	Batch		Custom	X

Specifications: Plastic products per customer

Date of Order: x/xx/xx Date of Completion: x/xx/xx

Costs Charged to Job	Previous Months	Current Month	Cost Summary
Direct materials			
Direct labor			
Manufacturing overhead (of direct labor costs)			
Total Cost			
Units completed			
Product unit cost			

Chapter 21, SD 5. (Continued)

			Job Order K-5
	Job Order Cost Card		
	Zavala Manufacturing Company		
Customer K-5	**Batch**		**Custom** X
Specifications Plastic products per customer			
Date of Order x/xx/xx		**Date of Completion**	

Costs Charged to Job	Previous Months	Current Month	Cost Summary
Direct materials			
Direct labor			
Manufacturing overhead (of direct labor costs)			
Total Cost			
Units completed			
Product unit cost			

Chapter 21, SD 5. (Continued)

Materials Inventory			
Beg. Bal.		Job K–2	
Purchases		Job K–4	
		Job K–5	
End. Bal.			

Finished Goods Inventory			
Beg. Bal.		Job K–1	
Job K–2		Job K–2	
Job K–4			
End. Bal.			

Work in Process Inventory			
Beg. Bal.		Job K–2	
Direct materials		Job K–4	
Direct labor			
Overhead			
End. Bal.			

Cost of Goods Sold			
Beg. Bal.			
Job K–1			
Job K–2			
End. Bal.			

3. Recommendations outlined

a.

b.

c.

Chapter 21, MRA 4.

1. Process cost report with schedule of equivalent production, unit cost analysis schedule, and cost summary schedule prepared

Seader Corporation
Shaping Department
Process Cost Report
For the Month Ended June 30, 20x5

1a. Schedule of equivalent production

Units—Stage of Completion	Units to Be Accounted For	Equivalent Units Direct Materials Costs	Equivalent Units Conversion Costs
Beginning inventory—units started last period but completed in this period			
Direct materials costs—100% complete			
Conversion costs—70% complete			
(x)			
Units started and completed in this period			
(–)			
Ending inventory—units started but not completed in this period			
Direct materials costs—100% complete			
Conversion costs—60% complete			
(x)			
Totals			

Chapter 21, MRA 4. (Continued)

1b. Unit cost analysis schedule

Total Cost Analysis	Costs from Beginning Inventory	Current Period Costs	Total Costs to Be Accounted For
Direct materials costs			
Conversion costs			
Totals			

Computation of Equivalent Unit Costs	Current Period Costs	÷ Equivalent Units	= Cost per Equivalent Unit
Direct materials costs			
Conversion costs			*
Totals			

*Rounded.

Chapter 21, MRA 4. (Continued)

1c. Cost summary schedule

	Cost of Goods Transferred to Finished Goods Inventory	Cost of Ending Work in Process Inventory	Total Costs to Be Accounted For
Beginning inventory			
Beginning balance		*	
Cost to complete:			
_____ units x _____ per unit			
Total beginning inventory			
Units started and completed			
_____ units x _____ per unit			
Ending inventory			
Direct materials costs:			
_____ units x _____ per unit			
Conversion costs:			
_____ units x _____ per unit			
Totals			

*(1.8 x _____) + (_____ x _____ x 70%) = _____ + _____

2. The amount of _____ should be transferred to the Finished Goods Inventory account.

3. The most significant change in the product costing information is _____

  1. _____
  2. _____
  3. _____
  4. _____

The production manager should explore each of these possible causes.

Chapter 22, SE 1.

Chapter 22, SE 2.

Chapter 22, SE 3.

Chapter 22, SE 4.
1.
2.
3.
4.
5.
6.

Chapter 22, SE 5.
1.
2.
3.

Chapter 22, SE 6.
1.
2.
3.
4.

Chapter 22, SE 7.

Chapter 22, SE 8.

1.
2.
3.
4.
5.
6.

Chapter 22, SE 9.

Chapter 22, SE 10.

Chapter 22, E 1.

Chapter 22, E 2.

1.	5.
2.	6.
3.	7.
4.	

Chapter 22, E 3.

1.	4.
2.	5.
3.	6.

Chapter 22, E 4.

Chapter 22, E 5.

1.	5.
2.	6.
3.	7.
4.	

Chapter 22, E 6.

*UL on special system orders.

Chapter 22, E 7.

Alachua Corporation
Bill of Activities
Union LLC Order

Activity	Activity Cost Rate	Cost Driver Level	Activity Cost
Unit level			
Parts production	per machine hour	machine hours	
Assembly	per direct labor hour	labor hours	
Packaging and shipping	per unit	units	
Batch level			
Work cell setup	per setup	setups	
Product level			
Product design	per engineering hour	engineering hours	
Product simulation	per testing hour	testing hours	
Facility level			
Building occupancy	of direct labor cost	direct labor cost	
Total activity costs assigned to job			
Total units of job			
Activity costs per unit (total activity costs ÷ total units)			
Cost Summary			
Direct materials			
Purchased parts			
Direct labor			
Activity costs			
Total cost of order			
Product unit cost (total cost ÷ 400 units)			

Chapter 22, E 8.

Materials handling cost rate computed

Direct materials:					
Cloth					
Fasteners					
Purchased parts					
Total materials cost					
Materials handling:					
Labor					
Equipment depreciation					
Electrical power					
Maintenance					
Total materials handling cost					
Materials handling cost rate					
	÷		=	per dollar of materials	

Design cost rate computed

Design:					
Labor					
Electrical power					
Overhead					
Total design cost					
Design cost rate					
	÷		=	per unit	

Chapter 22, E 9.

1.		5.	
2.		6.	
3.		7.	
4.			

Chapter 22, E 10.

1.		5.	
2.		6.	
3.		7.	
4.			

Chapter 22, E 11.

1 and 2. Costs in a traditional manufacturing setting and a JIT environment identified

	Traditional Setting	Costs That Are the Same in Both JIT and Traditional Settings	Costs That Change in a JIT Environment	Reason for the Change
Direct materials				
Sheet steel				
Iron castings				
Assembly parts				
Part 24RE6				
Part 15RF8				
Direct labor				
Engineering labor				
Indirect labor				
Operating supplies				
Small tools				
Depreciation, plant				
Depreciation, machinery				
Supervisory salaries				
Electrical power				
Insurance and taxes, plant				
President's salary				
Employee benefits				

Chapter 22, E 12.

Costs added to Cost of Goods Sold account:

Direct materials	
Conversion costs (direct labor and manufacturing overhead)	
Total manufacturing costs	
Less: Cost of goods completed	
Ending balance of Work in Process Inventory	
Cost of goods completed	
Less: Cost of goods sold	
Ending balance of Finished Goods Inventory	

Chapter 22, E 13.

Accounts Payable		Direct materials purchased and used		Cost of Goods Sold
		Conversion costs		
Conversion Costs		Costs remaining in Work in Process Inventory at month end backflushed		
		Work in Process Inventory		
Factory Payroll		Costs remaining in Finished Goods Inventory at month end backflushed		
		Finished Goods Inventory		
Manufacturing Overhead	*			

The total cost of goods sold for March is

| * | x | $17 |

Chapter 22, E 14.

1.
2.
3.
4.
5.

Chapter 22, E 15.

Manager 1:
Manager 2:

Chapter 22, P 1.

1. Nonvalue-adding activities identified

2. Value-adding activities grouped into the seven categories of the value chain

Marketing:	
Research and development:	
Purchasing:	
Production:	
Sales:	
Shipping:	
Customer service:	

3. Necessary and unnecessary nonvalue-adding activities identified

Materials moving:	
Product inspection:	
Materials storage:	
Materials inspection:	
Product rework:	
Finished goods storage:	

Chapter 22, P 2.

1. Traditional costing approach applied to job

Shawl Order:
- Direct materials
- Purchased parts
- Direct labor
- Manufacturing overhead (240% of direct labor cost)
- Total cost of order
- Product unit cost (total cost ÷ 150 units)

2. Cost hierarchy identified

Unit level:	
Batch level:	
Product level:	
Facility level:	

Chapter 22, P 2. (Continued)

3 and 4. Bill of activities prepared and activity-based costing applied to job

Boudreau Products, Inc.
Bill of Activities
Shawl Order

Activity	Activity Cost Rate	Cost Driver Level	Activity Cost
Unit level			
Parts production	per machine hour	machine hours	
Product assembly	per labor hour	labor hours	
Packaging	per package	packages	
Batch level			
Setup	per setup	setups	
Product level			
Engineering			
systems design	per engineering hour	engineering hours	
Facility level			
Building occupancy	per machine hour	machine hours	
Total activity costs assigned to job			
Total units of job			
Activity costs per unit (total activity costs ÷ total units)			
Cost summary			
Direct materials			
Purchased parts			
Direct labor			
Activity costs			
Total cost of order			
Product unit cost (total cost ÷ 150 units)			

5. Costs compared

Product unit cost—traditional costing	
Product unit cost—activity-based costing	
Difference	

In this case, the product unit cost computed using the traditional costing approach is lower than that computed using ABC. Activity-based costing does not guarantee cost reduction for every product. It does improve cost traceability, however, which often identifies products that have been undercosted or overcosted by a traditional product costing system.

Chapter 22, P 3.

1. Activity cost rates computed

a. Materials handling cost rate

    Direct materials:
- Leather
- Metal frame
- Bolts
- Total direct materials cost

    Materials handling:
- Labor
- Equipment depreciation
- Electrical power
- Maintenance
- Total materials handling cost

Materials handling cost rate

____ ÷ ____ = ____ per dollar of materials

b. Engineering design cost rate computed

    Engineering design:
- Labor
- Electrical power
- Engineering overhead
- Total engineering design cost

Engineering design cost rate

____ ÷ ____ = ____ per unit

Chapter 22, P 3. (Continued)

c.	Overhead rate computed						
	Overhead:						
		Equipment depreciation					
		Indirect labor					
		Supervision					
		Operating supplies					
		Electrical power					
		Repairs and maintenance					
		Building occupancy overhead					
		Total overhead cost					
	Machine hours						
			x	hours per unit	=		machine hours
	Overhead rate						
			÷		=		per machine hour

Chapter 22, P 3. (Continued)

2 and 3. Bill of activities prepared and activity-based costing applied to Job 142

Green Company
Bill of Activities
Job 142

Activity	Activity Cost Rate	Cost Driver Level	Activity Cost
Unit level			
Materials handling	per dollar of materials	materials	
Batch level			
None			
Product level			
Engineering design	per unit	units	
Facility level			
Overhead	per machine hour	machine hours	
		(3 MH × 500 units)	
Total activity costs assigned to job			
Total units of job			
Activity costs per unit (total activity costs ÷ total units)			
Cost summary			
Direct materials			
Direct labor			
Activity costs			
Total cost of order			
Product unit cost (total cost ÷ 500 units)			

Chapter 22, P 4.

1 and 2. Costs in a traditional manufacturing setting and a JIT environment identified

	Traditional Setting	JIT Environment
Wood		
Bolts		
Small tools		
Depreciation, plant		
Depreciation, machinery		
Direct labor		
Indirect labor		
Purchased parts		
Materials handling		
Insurance, plant		
President's salary		
Engineering labor		
Utilities		
Building occupancy		
Supervision		
Operating supplies		
Repairs and maintenance		
Employee benefits		

Chapter 22, P 4. (Continued)

3. Total direct cost and direct cost per unit computed for bridges produced in Toy Bridge work cell

Wood	
Bolts	
Small tools	
Depreciation, machinery	
Direct labor	
Indirect labor	
Purchased parts	
Materials handling	
Engineering labor	
Utilities	
Supervision	
Operating supplies	
Repairs and maintenance	
Employee benefits	
Total direct cost, Toy Bridge work cell	
Total units	
Direct cost per unit	

Chapter 22, P 5.

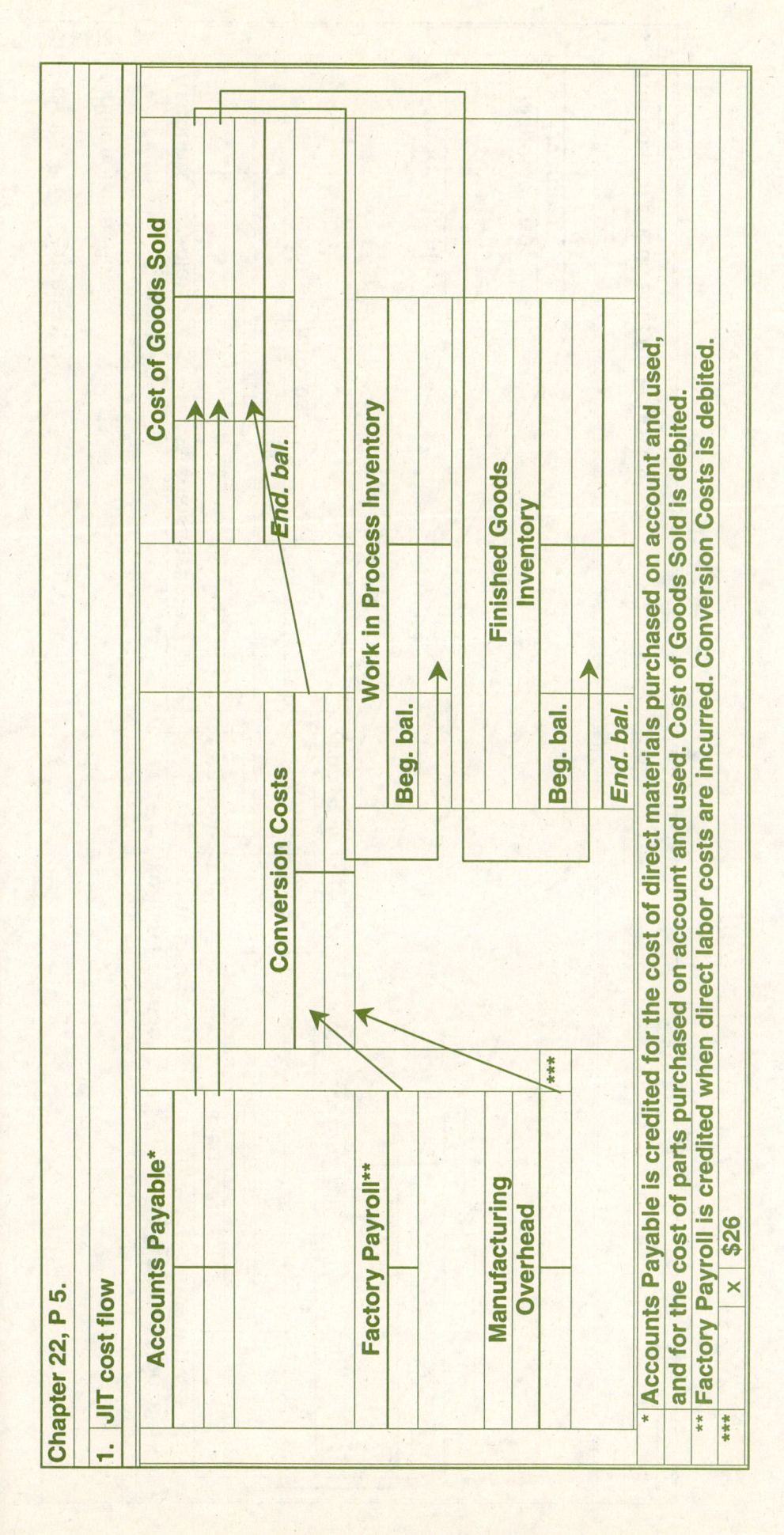

1. JIT cost flow

Accounts Payable*

Conversion Costs

Cost of Goods Sold

End. bal.

Work in Process Inventory

Beg. bal.

Finished Goods Inventory

Beg. bal.

End. bal.

Factory Payroll**

Manufacturing Overhead

***

* Accounts Payable is credited for the cost of direct materials purchased on account and used, and for the cost of parts purchased on account and used. Cost of Goods Sold is debited.

** Factory Payroll is credited when direct labor costs are incurred. Conversion Costs is debited.

*** x $26

Chapter 22, P 5. (Continued)

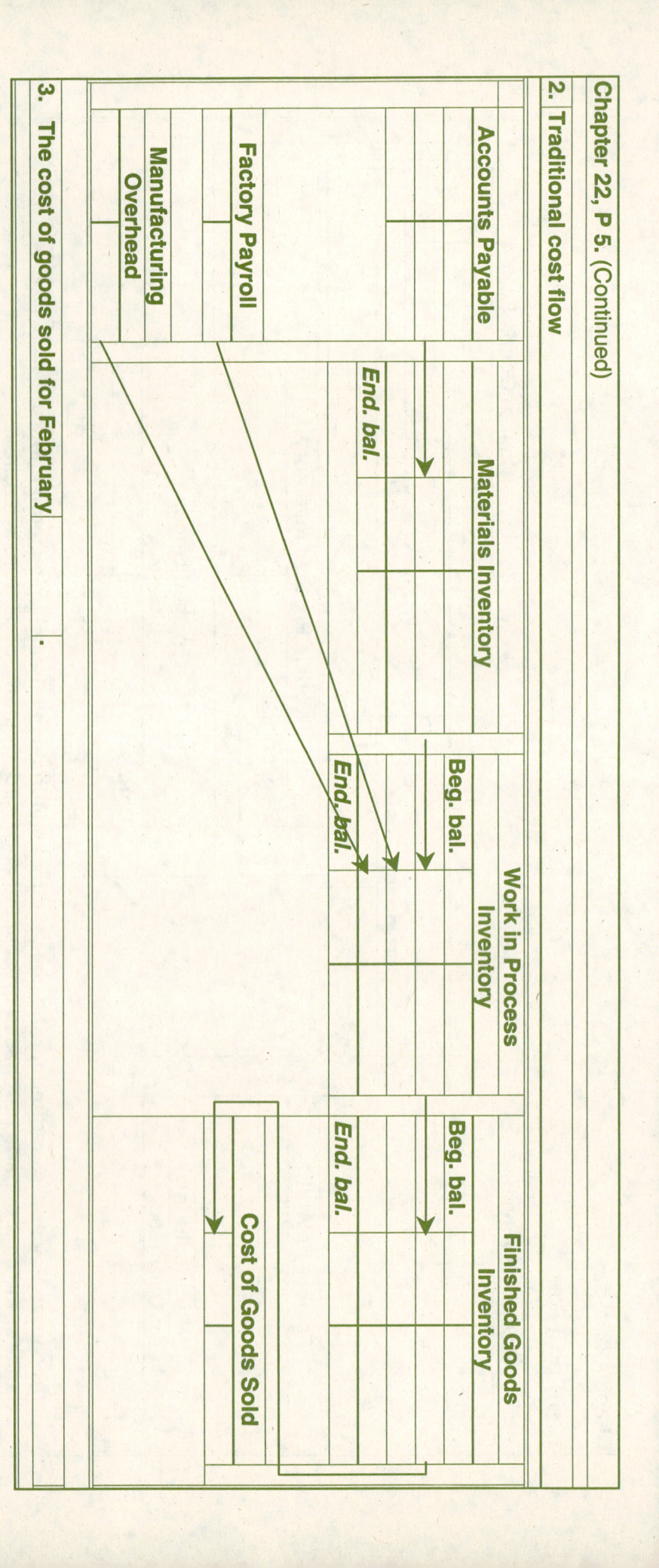

2. Traditional cost flow

Accounts Payable		Materials Inventory			Work in Process Inventory			Finished Goods Inventory	
			End. bal.		Beg. bal.			Beg. bal.	End. bal.
					End. bal.				

Factory Payroll			

Manufacturing Overhead		

Cost of Goods Sold

3. The cost of goods sold for February _____.

Chapter 22, P 6.

1. Traditional costing approach applied to job

Many Maids Order:			
Direct materials			
Purchased parts			
Direct labor			
Manufacturing overhead (	of direct labor cost)		
Total cost of order			
Product unit cost (total cost ÷	units)		

2. Cost hierarchy identified

Unit level:	
Batch level:	
Product level:	
Facility level:	

Chapter 22, P 6. (Continued)

3 and 4. Bill of activities prepared and activity-based costing applied to job

<table>
<tr><td colspan="4" align="center">Mau Cellular Company
Bill of Activities
Many Maids Order</td></tr>
<tr><th>Activity</th><th>Activity Cost Rate</th><th>Cost Driver Level</th><th>Activity Cost</th></tr>
<tr><td>**Unit level**</td><td></td><td></td><td></td></tr>
<tr><td>   Parts production</td><td>per machine hour</td><td>machine hours</td><td></td></tr>
<tr><td>   Packaging</td><td>per package</td><td>packages</td><td></td></tr>
<tr><td>**Batch level**</td><td></td><td></td><td></td></tr>
<tr><td>   Setup</td><td>per setup</td><td>setups</td><td></td></tr>
<tr><td>**Product level**</td><td></td><td></td><td></td></tr>
<tr><td>   Electrical engineering design</td><td>per engineering hour</td><td>engineering hours</td><td></td></tr>
<tr><td>   Product testing</td><td>per test</td><td>tests</td><td></td></tr>
<tr><td>**Facility level**</td><td></td><td></td><td></td></tr>
<tr><td>   Building occupancy</td><td>per machine hour</td><td>machine hours</td><td>*</td></tr>
<tr><td>Total activity costs assigned to job</td><td></td><td></td><td></td></tr>
<tr><td>Total units of job</td><td></td><td></td><td></td></tr>
<tr><td>Activity costs per unit (total activity costs ÷ total units)</td><td></td><td></td><td></td></tr>
<tr><td>**Cost summary**</td><td></td><td></td><td></td></tr>
<tr><td>   Direct materials</td><td></td><td></td><td></td></tr>
<tr><td>   Purchased parts</td><td></td><td></td><td></td></tr>
<tr><td>   Direct labor</td><td></td><td></td><td></td></tr>
<tr><td>   Activity costs</td><td></td><td></td><td></td></tr>
<tr><td>   Total cost of order</td><td></td><td></td><td></td></tr>
<tr><td>   Product unit cost (total cost ÷ 80 units)</td><td></td><td></td><td></td></tr>
</table>

*Rounded.

5. Costs compared

Product unit cost—traditional costing	
Product unit cost—activity-based costing	
Difference	

In this case, the ABC product unit cost is lower than that computed using the traditional costing approach. Activity-based costing does not guarantee cost reduction for every product. It does improve cost traceability, however, which often identifies products that have been undercosted or overcosted by a traditional product costing system.

Chapter 22, P 7.

1. Activity cost rates computed

a. Materials handling cost rate

Direct materials:
- Aluminum frame
- Bolts
- Total direct materials cost

Materials handling:
- Labor
- Utilities
- Maintenance
- Depreciation
- Total materials handling cost

Materials handling cost rate:

_____ ÷ _____ = _____ per dollar of materials

b. Setup cost rate

Setup:
- Labor
- Supplies
- Overhead
- Total setup cost

Setup cost rate:

_____ ÷ _____ setups = _____ per setup

Chapter 22, P 7. (Continued)

c. Product testing cost rate

    Product testing:
        Labor
        Supplies
        Total product testing cost

    Product testing cost rate:

        ÷   tests = per test

d. Building occupancy cost rate

    Building occupancy:
        Insurance
        Depreciation
        Repairs and maintenance
        Total building occupancy cost

    Building occupancy cost rate:

        ÷   machine hours = per machine hour

Chapter 22, P 7. (Continued)

2 and 3. Bill of activities prepared and activity-based costing applied to job

Benning Company
Bill of Activities
Executive Toys Job

Activity	Activity Cost Rate	Cost Driver Level	Activity Cost
Unit level			
Materials handling	per dollar of materials	materials	
Batch level			
Setup	per setup	setups	
Product level			
Product testing	per test	tests	
Facility level			
Building occupancy	per machine hour	machine hours	
Total activity costs assigned to job			
Total units of job			
Activity costs per unit (	÷	)	
Cost summary			
Direct materials			
Purchased parts			
Direct labor			
Activity costs			
Total cost of job			
Product unit cost (	÷	)	

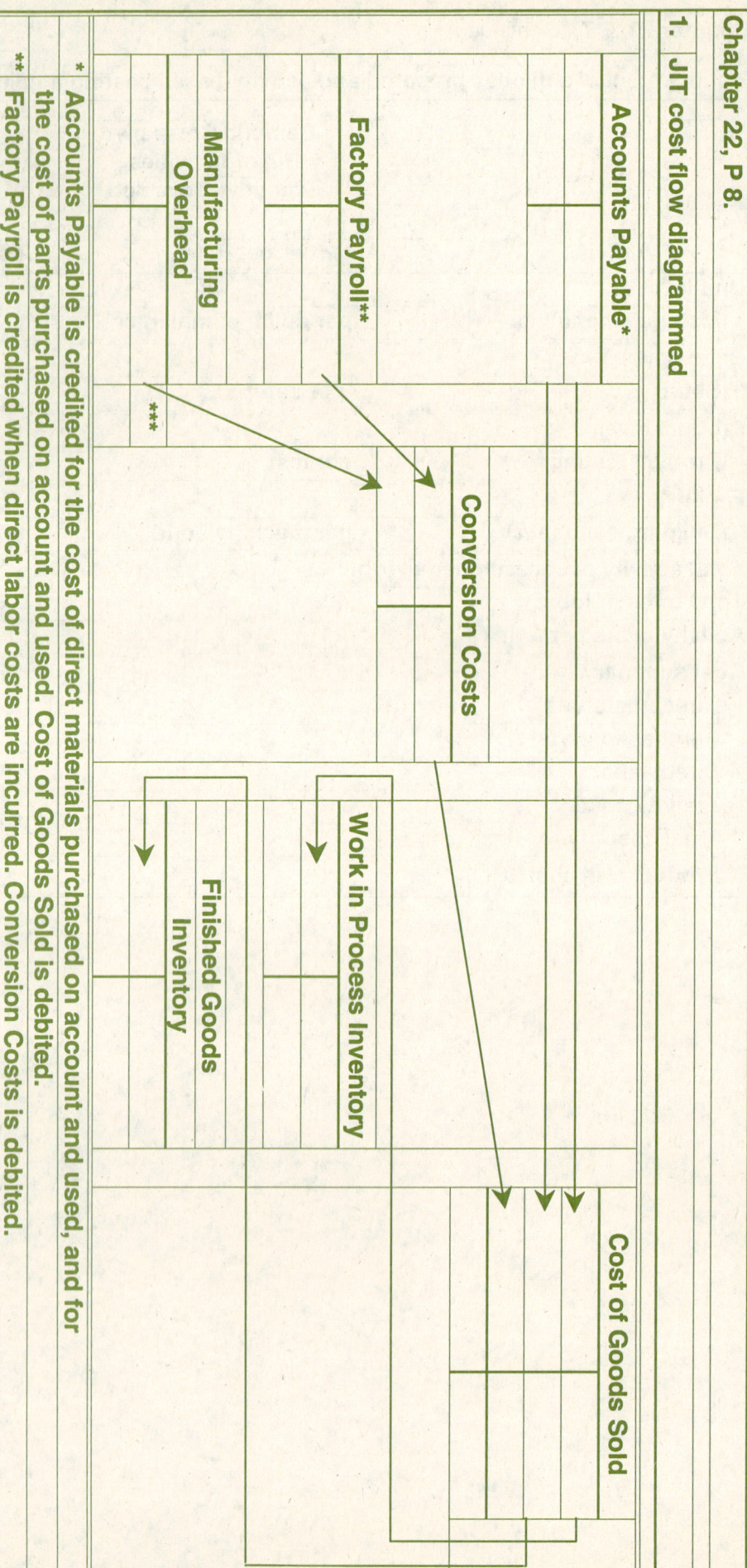

Chapter 22, P 8.

1. JIT cost flow diagrammed

Accounts Payable*		Conversion Costs		Cost of Goods Sold
Factory Payroll**		Work in Process Inventory		
Manufacturing Overhead		Finished Goods Inventory		

* Accounts Payable is credited for the cost of direct materials purchased on account and used, and for the cost of parts purchased on account and used. Cost of Goods Sold is debited.

** Factory Payroll is credited when direct labor costs are incurred. Conversion Costs is debited.

*** × $14

Chapter 22, P 8. (Continued)

2. Traditional cost flow diagrammed

Accounts Payable	Materials Inventory	Work in Process Inventory	Finished Goods Inventory

Factory Payroll			Cost of Goods Sold

Manufacturing Overhead

3. The cost of goods sold for April is _____.

Chapter 22, MRA 1.

1. Planned activity costs calculated

Activity	Planned Activity Cost Rate	Planned Annual Cost Driver Level	Planned Activity Cost
Make sales calls	per sales call	sales calls	
Prepare sales orders	per sales order	sales orders	
Handle inquiries	per minute	minutes	
Ship products	per case sold	cases	
Process invoices	per invoice	invoices	
Process credit	per notice	notices	
Process billings and collections	per billing	billings	
Total			

2. Differences between planned and State Prisons customer group's activity costs computed

Activity	Planned Activity Cost	State Prisons Customer Group Activity Cost	Difference Under (Over)
Make sales calls			
Prepare sales orders			
Handle inquiries			
Ship products			
Process invoices			
Process credit			
Process billings and collections			
Totals			

Chapter 22, MRA 1. (Continued)

3. Nonvalue-adding activities identified

4. Actions to reduce nonvalue-adding activities suggested

Chapter 22, MRA 3.

1 and 2.

	Traditional Costing Approach	Activity-Based Costing Approach
Total direct labor costs		
Other direct costs		
Overhead costs		
(Traditional approach: _____ x 120%)		
Cost of activities:		
Professional development		
(_____ per employee x _____ employees)		
Administration		
(_____ per job x _____ jobs)		
Client development		
(_____ per new client x _____ new clients)		
Total costs assigned to the audit function		
Average cost per audit job		

3. Difference in total costs computed and discussed

Chapter 22, MRA 4.

1. Budgeted income statement prepared

Star Bakery
Budgeted Income Statement for State Prisons Customer Group
For the year ending December 31, 20x1

Sales

| | per case | × | | cases) | | |

Cost of goods sold

| (| per case | × | | cases) | | |

Gross margin

Less: Selling and administrative activities costs

Activity	Activity Cost Rate	Cost Driver Level	Activity Cost
Make sales calls	per sales call	sales calls	
Prepare sales orders	per sales order	sales orders	
Handle inquiries	per minute	minutes	
Ship products	per case sold	cases	
Customer service agency	of sales revenue	sales	
Total selling and administrative costs			

Net income contributed by State Prisons customer group

Chapter 22, MRA 4. (Continued)

2. Planned activity costs calculated

Activity	Planned Activity Cost Rate	Planned Annual Cost Driver Level	Planned Activity Cost
Make sales calls	per sales call	sales calls	
Prepare sales orders	per sales order	sales orders	
Handle inquiries	per minute	minutes	
Ship products	per case sold	cases	
Process invoices	per invoice	invoices	
Process credit	per notice	notices	
Process billings and collections	per billing	billings	
Total			

Chapter 22, MRA 4. (Continued)

3. Differences between planned and State Prisons customer group's activity costs computed

Activity	Planned Activity Cost	State Prisons Customer Group Activity Cost	Difference Under (Over)
Make sales calls			
Prepare sales orders			
Handle inquiries			
Ship products			
Process invoices			
Process credit			
Process billings and collections			
Customer service agency			
Totals			

4.

Chapter 23, SE 1.

Hat maker A:
    Variable cost per derby
    Fixed cost per derby (÷   )

Hat maker B:
    Variable cost per derby
    Fixed cost per derby (÷   )

Chapter 23, SE 2.

1.
2.
3.
4.
5.

Chapter 23, SE 3.

Volume	Month	Activity Level	Cost
High	June	hours	
Low	May	hours	
Difference		hours	

Variable cost per telephone hour =   ÷ 12 hours
    =   per hour

Fixed cost for June =   − (×   ) =
Fixed cost for May =   − (×   ) =

Chapter 23, SE 4.

Sales Revenue	=	Variable Costs	+	Fixed Costs	+	Profit
x	=	(x)	+		+	
x	=					
x	=					

Chapter 23, SE 5.

	x	=	x	+		
	x	=				
	x	=	Units			
Breakeven Dollars	=	x	Units	=		

Chapter 23, SE 6.

Breakeven Units	=	Fixed Costs	÷	Contribution Margin per Unit
	=		÷	(−)
	=		÷	
	=	Units		

Chapter 23, SE 7.

Contribution Margin Ratio	=	Contribution Margin / Selling Price	=	*	=	
Breakeven Dollars	=	Fixed Costs / Contribution Margin Ratio	=		=	
*	−		=			

Chapter 23, SE 8.

	Sales	−	Variable Costs	=	Contribution Margin (CM)	x	Sales Mix	=	Weighted-Average CM
A		−		=		x	0.667	=	
B		−		=		x		=	
	Weighted-average contribution margin								

| Weighted-Average Breakeven Point = | | ÷ | | = | | Units |

Breakeven point for each product line:

	Weighted-Average Breakeven Point		Sales Mix	=	Breakeven Point	
A	=	Units	x	0.667	=	Units
B	=	Units	x	0.000	=	Units

Check: Contribution margin

Product A	=		x		=	
Product B	=		x		=	
Total contribution margin	
Less fixed costs	
Profit	

Chapter 23, SE 9.

	Profit	=	Contribution Margin		−	Fixed Costs	
	Profit	=	(	−	)	−	
		=	(	)		−	
		=		−			
		=					

Chapter 23, SE 10.

Volume		Month	Activity Level		Cost
Highest		November		cases	
Lowest		December		cases	
Difference				cases	
Variable Cost per Case	=	÷	Cases	=	per Case
Fixed Cost for November	=	− (	x	) =	
Fixed Cost for December	=	− (	x	) =	
Variable cost per case for December					
Direct labor					
Variable service overhead					
Variable cost per case					
Fixed cost per case for December					
Fixed service overhead	(	+	)		

Chapter 23, E 1.

1.		9.	
2.		10.	
3.		11.	
4.		12.	
5.		13.	
6.		14.	
7.		15.	
8.		16.	

Chapter 23, E 2.

1. Cost of oil computed

Month	Cars to Be Serviced	Required Quarts/Car	Cost/Quart	Total Cost/Month
1				
2				
3				
Three-month total				

2. Information about cost behavior provided

Cost per unit			
Total variable cost per month			as the quantity of oil used

Chapter 23, E 3.

1. Variable electricity cost per machine hour computed

Volume	Month	Machine Hours	Electricity Cost	
Highest	July			
Lowest	December			
Difference				
Variable Rate	=	÷	=	per Machine Hour

2. Monthly fixed electricity cost computed

July:		− (	x	)
	=		Fixed Electricity Cost	
December:		− (	x	)
	=		Fixed Electricity Cost	

3. Total variable and fixed electricity costs for six months computed

Total variable costs				
(	—	machine hours x	per machine hour)	
Total fixed costs				
($	—	x	months)	
Total electricity costs for six months				

Chapter 23, E 4.

1.
2.
3.
4.
5.
6.

Chapter 23, E 5.

1. Breakeven units computed

$$\text{BE Units} = \frac{FC}{\text{CM per Unit}}$$

$$= \frac{ + }{ - (+)}$$

$$= $$

$$= \text{Sets}$$

2. Breakeven dollars computed

BE Dollars	=	BE Units	×	Selling Price per Set
	=		×	
	=			

3. New breakeven units computed

$$\text{BE Units} = \frac{FC}{\text{CM per Unit}}$$

$$= \frac{ + }{ - (+)}$$

$$= $$

$$= \text{Sets}$$

Chapter 23, E 5. (Continued)

4. Breakeven graph prepared

Units	Fixed Costs	Variable Costs*	Total Costs	Total Sales**
—				
5,000				
10,000				
15,000				
20,000				
25,000				
30,000				
35,000				
40,000				

* Variable Costs per Unit = ___ + ___ = ___

** Sales = ___ per Unit Sold

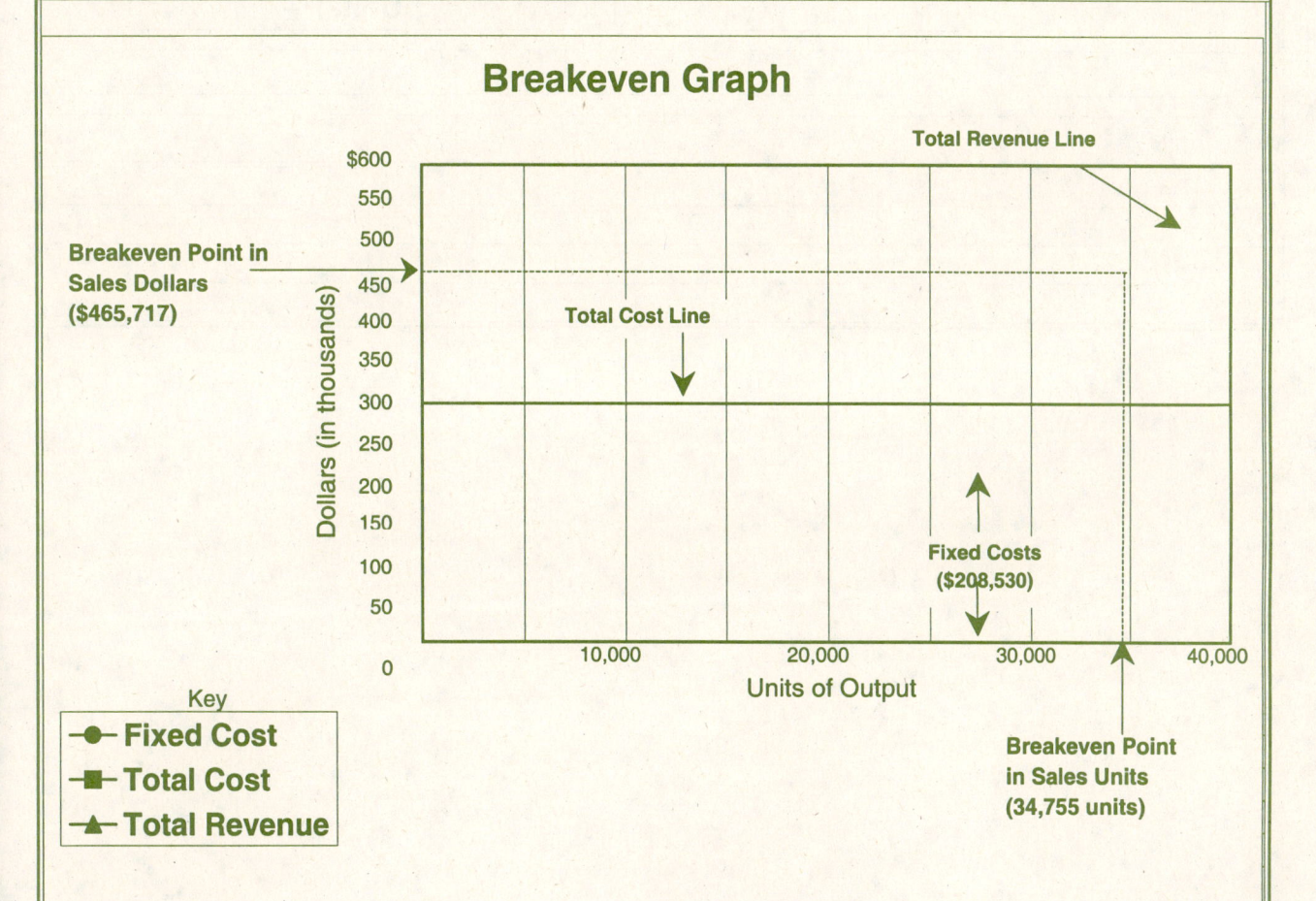

Breakeven Graph

Breakeven Point in Sales Dollars ($465,717)

Total Revenue Line

Total Cost Line

Fixed Costs ($208,530)

Breakeven Point in Sales Units (34,755 units)

Y-axis: Dollars (in thousands), 0 to $600
X-axis: Units of Output, 10,000 to 40,000

Key:
- Fixed Cost
- Total Cost
- Total Revenue

Chapter 23, E 6.

1. Breakeven computed

| BE Units | = | | = | | * | = | | Units |

| * | SP per Unit | = | |

| FC | = | | + | | = | |

| VC per Unit | = | | + | | + | | = | |
| | | | Units | | | | | |

| CM per Unit | = | SP per Unit − VC per Unit | = | | − | | = | |

2. New profit computed and recommendation made

CM per Unit	=	SP per Unit − VC per Unit	=		−		=	
Projected Operating Income	=	(CM per Unit x Sales Forecast) − FC
	=	(	x	Units) −
	=		−	
	=			

Chapter 23, E 7.

	Sales	−	Variable Costs	=	Contribution Margin (CM)	x	Percentage of Sales Mix	=	Weighted-Average CM
Aquariums		−		=		x		=	
Water pumps		−		=		x		=	
Air filters		−		=		x		=	
Weighted-average contribution margin									
Weighted-Average Breakeven Point			=		+		=		Units

Breakeven point for each product:

Aquariums		units	x		=		units
Water pumps		units	x		=		units
Air filters		units	x		=		units

Check: Contribution margin

Aquariums	=		x		=	
Water pumps	=		x		=	
Air filters	=		x		=	
Total contribution margin						
Less fixed costs						
Profit						

Chapter 23, E 8.

	Contribution Margin (CM)/Unit	x	Percentage of Sales Mix	=	Weighted-Average CM	
Shampoo and set		x		=		
Permanents		x		=		
Cut and blow dry		x		=		
Weighted-average contribution margin						
Weighted-Average Breakeven Point	=		÷		=	Units

Breakeven point for each product:

Shampoo and set		units	x		=	units
Permanents		units	x		=	units
Cut and blow dry		units	x		=	units

Check: Contribution margin

Shampoo and set	=		x		=
Permanents	=		x		=
Cut and blow dry	=		x		=
Total contribution margin					
Less fixed costs					
Profit					

Chapter 23, E 9.

1. Target sales units calculated

Target Sales Units	=					
	=		+			
			−			
	=					
	=	Units				

2. Revised target sales units calculated

Target Sales Units	=					
	=	(	+	) +		
		− (	−	)		
	=		+			
			−			
	=					
	=	* Units				

*Rounded.

Chapter 23, E 9. (Continued)

3. Additional units needed to earn higher profit calculated

Additional Units = ⎯⎯⎯⎯⎯⎯

= ⎯⎯⎯⎯⎯⎯

= _____ Units

Proof:

Target Sales Units = ⎯⎯⎯⎯⎯⎯

= ⎯⎯⎯⎯⎯ + ⎯⎯⎯⎯⎯

= ⎯⎯⎯⎯⎯⎯

= _____ * Units

*Rounded.

Chapter 23, E 10.

1. Target sales units calculated

Target Sales Units	=	
	=	___ + ___ / ___ − ___
	=	
	=	_____ Daily Rentals

2. Target average number of rental days per auto per year computed

	Daily Rentals	÷	Autos	=	* Days per Auto per Year

*Rounded.

3. Target sales dollars computed

Target Sales Dollars	=	Number of Daily Rentals	x	Rental per Auto
	=	___ x ___		
	=			

4. Revised target sales dollars computed

Revised Target Sales Dollars	=	[(FC + P) / CM per Unit]	x	Selling Price
	=	[(___ − ___) + ___]	x	
	=	[___ + ___]	x	
	=	[___]	x	
	=			

Chapter 23, E 11.

1. Variable and fixed cost components calculated

Using the high-low method:

Volume	Month	Number of Tax Returns	Cost
Highest	February		
Lowest	March		
Difference			

Variable Overhead Rate = _____ ÷ _____ Tax Returns = _____ per Tax Return

Fixed Service Overhead Costs	=	Total Service Overhead Costs	−	Variable Service Overhead Costs	
	=		− (	×	)
	=				

2. Estimated total cost per tax return in April calculated

Direct professional labor				
Variable service overhead				
Fixed service overhead	(_____ ÷ _____ tax returns)			*
Estimated total cost per tax return				

*Rounded.

Chapter 23, E 12.

	Let x	=	Sales in Units		
	S	=	VC + FC + P		
	x	=	x +		+
	x	=			
	x	=	Inspections		

Chapter 23, P 1.

1. Costs classified

Variable costs:

Fixed costs:

Mixed costs:

2. High-low method applied

Volume		Month	Number of Jobs	Utilities Cost
Highest		August		
Lowest		March		
Difference				

Variable Rate per Job	=	———	=	
Monthly Fixed Cost	=		− (x)	
	=		−	
	=			

Chapter 23, P 1. (Continued)

3 and 4. Projected total costs and projected cost per job computed

							Total Cost	Cost per Job
Variable costs:								
Labor	(	jobs	×	hours	×	per hour)		
Tars-Off	(	jobs	×			per can)		
Buff Glow	[	jobs	× (	lbs	×	per lb ÷	jobs)]	
Poly Wax	[	jobs	× (	lbs	×	per lb ÷	jobs)]	
Fixed costs:								
Rent	(		×	months)				
Mixed costs:								
Utilities	[(	jobs	×	) + (	×	months)]		
Totals								*
								*

*Rounded.

5. Decision about raising the price discussed

Chapter 23, P 2.

1. Breakeven units computed

BE Units	=	FC ÷ CM per Unit
	=	÷ (−)
	=	÷
	=	Systems

2. Breakeven dollars computed

BE Dollars	=	BE Units × Selling Price per Unit
	=	×
	=	

3. Breakeven units revised based on higher fixed costs

BE Units	=	FC ÷ CM per Unit
	=	(+) ÷ (−)
	=	÷
	=	Systems

4. Breakeven units revised based on new operating data

BE Units	=	FC ÷ CM per Unit
	=	(+) ÷ [− (−)]
	=	÷ (−)
	=	÷
	=	Systems

Chapter 23, P 3.

1a. Breakeven units computed

BE Units	=	FC ÷ CM per Unit					
	=	*	÷ (		−	**	)
	=		÷				
	=		Units				

*		+		+		=	
**		+	+		+		+	=

1b. Target units computed

Target Sales Units	=	(FC + P) ÷ CM per Unit		
	=	(	+	) ÷
	=	÷		
	=	Units		

2. Breakeven units revised based on new operating data

Target Sales Units	=	(FC + P) ÷ CM per Unit			
	=	(	+	+	) ÷
	=	÷			
	=	Units			

3. Selling price determined

Target Sales Units	=	(FC + P) ÷ CM per Unit		
	=	(	+	) ÷ CM per Unit

Multiplying both sides of the equation by CM per Unit, we get

	x CM per Unit	=	
	CM per Unit	=	
Revised SP per Unit	=	CM per Unit + VC per Unit	
Revised SP per Unit	=	+	=

Chapter 23, P 3. (Continued)

4. Increased advertising costs determined

		=	(FC	+		) + (		–		)
		=	(FC	+		) + (		)		

Multiplying both sides of the equation by $8.75, we get

	(		)	=	FC	+			
		FC	=		(		)	–	
		FC	=			–			
		FC	=						

Total fixed costs allowed	
Less original fixed cost estimate	
Additional dollars available for advertising	

Chapter 23, P 4.

1a and 1b. Breakeven units and dollars computed

BE Units	=	FC / CM per Unit
	=	(+) / (− (+))
	=	
	=	Units
BE Dollars	=	Units ×
	=	

2. Target sales units computed

Target Sales Units	=	(FC + P) / CM per Unit
	=	(+) /
	=	
	=	Units

Chapter 23, P 4. (Continued)

3. Contribution margin per unit computed

a. SP − VC per Unit = CM per Unit × Units = Fixed Costs Covered

	−		=		×		=	

b. $\dfrac{FC + P}{Units}$ = CM per Unit

$$= \dfrac{(\quad - \quad) + \quad}{Units}$$

= _____

= CM per Unit Required on Remaining Units

Required contribution margin (	+	)	
Less contribution margin already generated			
(	Units ×	)	
Balance of contribution margin to be generated			

$$\dfrac{\text{Required CM per Unit}}{\text{on Balance of Sales}} = \dfrac{\text{Balance of CM to Be Generated}}{\text{Remaining Sales Volume}}$$

$$= \dfrac{\quad}{\quad - \quad}$$

= _____

= _____

Chapter 23, P 5.

1a. Breakeven number of applications computed

BE Units	=	FC ÷ CM per Loan
	=	(+ + +) / [− (×) − −]
	=	÷ = Loans

1b. Target number of applications computed

Target Sales Units	=	(FC + P) ÷ CM per Loan
	=	(+ + +) +
	=	÷ = Loans

2. Target number of applications computed based on new operating data

Target Sales Units	=	(FC + P) ÷ CM per Loan
	=	(+ + +) +
	=	÷ = Loans

Chapter 23, P 5. (Continued)

3. Application fee determined

	x	=	Loan Application Fee						
Target Revenue		=	VC + FC + P						
	x	=	(		×	500	) +	+	
	x	=	(	+			+	) ÷	
	x	=		÷					
	x	=							

4. Maximum additional promotional costs determined

		x	=	Maximum Additional Promotional Costs							
Target Revenue			=	VC + FC + P							
750	x		=	(	×	) +		+		+	x
			=		+		+		+	x	
			=		+	x					
	x		=		−						
	x		=								

Chapter 23, P 6.

1. Breakeven hours computed

BE Units	=	FC ÷ CM per Hour					
	=		÷ (		−		−	)
	=		÷	
	=		Billable Hours

2. Breakeven billings computed

BE Dollars	=	BE Hours × Billing Rate per Hour
	=	Hours ×
	=	

3. Breakeven billings revised based on higher fixed costs

BE Dollars	=	Billing Rate per Hour × (FC ÷ CM per Hour)
	=	(× [÷ (− −)]
	=	× (÷)
	=	×
	=	

4. Breakeven billings revised based on new operating data

BE Dollars	=	Billing Rate per Hour × (FC ÷ CM per Hour)
	=	(× [÷ (− −)]
	=	× (÷)
	=	×
	=	

Chapter 23, P 7.

1a. Breakeven units computed

BE Units	=	FC ÷ CM per Unit
	=	(+ +) ÷ [− (+ + + +)]
	=	÷ (−)
	=	÷
	=	Units

1b. Target units computed

Target Sales Units	=	(FC + P) ÷ CM per Unit
	=	(+) ÷
	=	÷
	=	Units

2. Target sales units revised based on new operating data

Target Sales Units	=	(FC + P) ÷ CM per Unit
	=	(+ +) ÷
	=	÷
	=	Units

Chapter 23, P 7. (Continued)

3. Selling price determined

Target Sales Units	=	(FC + P) ÷ CM per Unit				
	=	(		+	) ÷ CM per Unit	

Multiplying both sides of the equation by CM per Unit, we get

	x	CM per Unit	=	
		CM per Unit	=	
	Revised SP per Unit	=	CM per Unit + VC per Unit	
	Revised SP per Unit	=	+	=

4. Increased advertising costs determined

Target Sales Units	=	(FC + P) ÷ CM per Unit			
	=	(FC +	) ÷ (	−	)
	=	(FC +	) ÷		

Multiplying both sides of the equation by $23.40, we get

(	)	=	FC +		
	FC	=	[(	) −	]
	FC	=	−		
	FC	=			

Total fixed costs allowed	
Less original fixed cost estimate	
Additional dollars available for advertising	

Chapter 23, P 8.

1. Costs classified

Variable costs:	Fixed costs:
	Mixed costs:

2. High-low method applied

Volume	Month	Hours Worked	Utilities Cost
Highest	August		
Lowest	February		
Difference			

Variable Rate = ⎯⎯⎯ = ⎯⎯⎯ per Hour Worked

Monthly Fixed Cost = ⎯⎯⎯ − (⎯⎯⎯ × ⎯⎯⎯)
 = ⎯⎯⎯ − ⎯⎯⎯
 = ⎯⎯⎯

3. Average cost per job calculated

Variable costs:

Skilled labor		×	12 × 628	=	
Unskilled labor		×	×	=	
Debris-Luse		×		=	
Paint primer		×		=	
Paint		×		=	

Fixed costs:

Depreciation, Lease, Rent	/mo. × 12 mos. =

Mixed costs:

Utilities

Average Cost per Job = ⎯⎯⎯ ÷ ⎯⎯⎯ Jobs
 = ⎯⎯⎯ per Job

Chapter 23, SD 5.

1. Variable cost rates for electricity and repairs computed

Electricity Expense:

	Cost	Kilowatt Hours Used	
Highest			
Lowest			
Difference			

Variable Rate = _____ ÷ _____ Hours = _____ per Kilowatt Hour

Fixed Cost = Total Cost − Variable Cost

| April: | _____ − (_____ × _____) = _____ Fixed Electricity Cost |
| July: | _____ − (_____ × _____) = _____ Fixed Electricity Cost |

Repairs and Maintenance Expense:

	Cost	Labor Hours Used	
Highest			
Lowest			
Difference			

Variable Rate = _____ ÷ _____ Hours = _____ per Labor Hour

Fixed Cost = Total Cost − Variable Cost

| September: | _____ − (_____ × _____) = _____ Fixed R & M Cost |
| April: | _____ − (_____ × _____) = _____ Fixed R & M Cost |

Chapter 23, SD 5. (Continued)

2. Total variable and fixed costs per category computed

Electricity Expense:
    Total variable cost:
        _____ kilowatt-hours x _____ per kilowatt-hour
    Total fixed cost:
        _____ x _____ months

Repairs and Maintenance Expense:
    Total variable cost:
        _____ labor hours x _____ per labor hour
    Total fixed cost:
        _____ x _____ months

3. Total cost for each category computed

Electricity Expense:
    Total variable cost:
        _____ kilowatt-hours x _____ per kilowatt-hour
    Total fixed cost:
        _____ x _____ months
    Total

Repairs and Maintenance Expense:
    Total variable cost:
        _____ labor hours x _____ per labor hour
    Total fixed cost:*
        _____ x _____ months
    Total

*Computed in part 2.

Chapter 23, MRA 1.

1. Relevant data per set of china calculated

a.	Selling Price per Set	=	Total Sales / Number of Sets Sold
		=	
		=	

b.	Variable Purchases Cost per Set	=	Total Variable Purchases Costs / Number of Sets Sold
		=	
		=	

c.	Variable Distribution Cost per Set	=	Total Variable Distribution Costs / Number of Sets Sold
		=	
		=	

d.	Variable Sales Commission per Set	=	Total Variable Sales Commissions / Number of Sets Sold
		=	
		=	

e. Selling price per set
Less:
    Variable purchases cost
    Variable distribution cost
    Variable sales commission
        Total variable costs per set
Contribution margin

Chapter 23, MRA 1. (Continued)

2. Breakeven point in units and in dollars calculated

BE Units	=	FC ÷ CM per Set
	=	
	=	Sets
BE Dollars	=	BE Sets × Selling Price per Set
	=	Sets ×
	=	

3. Ratio of variable costs to sales calculated and corrective actions discussed

Variable Cost Ratio	=	Variable Costs / Sales
	=	÷
	=	

To reduce variable costs, the following actions could be taken:

a.

b.

c.

d.

e.

f.

4.

Chapter 23, MRA 2.

1. Contribution income statement prepared

Nambe-Casa, Ltd.
Contribution Income Statement
For the Year Ended December 31, 20x2

Sales	(	sets x		)			
Less Variable Costs							
	Purchases						
	Distribution (	x		)			
	Sales Commissions						
	(0.12 x	x	)				
	Total Variable Costs						
Contribution Margin							
Less Fixed Costs							
	Distribution (0.90 x	)					
	Selling						
	General and Administrative						
	Total Fixed Costs						
Operating Income							

2. Questions answered

a.

b.

c.

d.

Chapter 23, MRA 4.

1.
2.
3.
4.
5.

Chapter 23, MRA 4. (Continued)

Parts 2, 3, and 4. Revised contribution margin statements prepared and contribution margin from Australian sales ca

Nambe-Casa, Ltd.
Revised Contribution Income Statements
For the Year Ended December 31, 20x2

	From MRA 2 Total Units	Per Unit	Australian Unit Sales	Per Unit	Revised Income Statement for Sales of Units
Sales					
Less Variable Costs					
Purchases					
Distribution					
Sales Commissions					
Total Variable Costs					
Contribution Margin					
Less Fixed Costs					
Distribution					
Selling					
General and Administrative					
Total Fixed Costs					
Operating Income					

Projected Operating Income	
Desired Operating Income Including 10% Increase over 20x1	(1.1 x)
Difference	

Chapter 24, SE 1.

1.
2.
3.
4.
5.

Chapter 24, SE 2.

Budgets that might be useful include:

1.
2.
3.
4.
5.

Chapter 24, SE 3.

Chapter 24, SE 4.

Chapter 24, SE 5.

Chapter 24, SE 6.

Salaries, sales representatives	(	3	x			)			
Sales commissions	(			units	x		x	5%)	
Sales brochures and supplies									
Travel expenses	(			miles	x			per mile)	
Total budgeted selling expenses									

Chapter 24, SE 7.

Net Sales				
Cost of Goods Sold				
Finished Goods Inventory, Beginning				
Cost of Goods Manufactured			*	
Total Cost of Goods Available for Sale				
Less Finished Goods Inventory, Ending				
Cost of Goods Sold				
Gross Margin				
* Cost of Goods Manufactured				
Direct Materials Used				
Materials Inventory, Beginning				
Purchases				
Cost of Direct Materials Available for Use				
Less Materials Inventory, Ending				
Cost of Direct Materials Used				
Direct Labor Costs				
Manufacturing Overhead Costs				
Total Manufacturing Costs				
Add Work in Process Inventory, Beginning				
Less Work in Process Inventory, Ending				
Cost of Goods Manufactured				

Chapter 24, SE 8.

May cash collections:

June	(	x	)			
May	(	x	)			
April	(	x	)			
March	(	x	)			
March penalty	(		x	)		
Total						

Chapter 24, SE 9.

Martinson Corp.
Schedule of Expected Cash Payments for Direct Materials
For the Quarter Ended March 31, 20x1

					January	February	March	Quarter
Cash Purchases								
Payments on credit purchases:								
December	(		x	0.40)				
January	(		x	)				
	(		x	)				
February	(		x	)				
	(		x	)				
March	(		x	)				

Chapter 24, SE 10.

Total assets			
Less:	Total liabilities		
	Common stock		
	Current year's income		
Beginning retained earnings			

Chapter 24, E 1.

1.
2.
3.
4.
5.
6.
7.
8.
9.
10.

Chapter 24, E 2.

1.
2.
3.
4.

Chapter 24, E 3.

1.
2.

Chapter 24, E 4.

In discussions with the president concerning the initial steps in the development of a budgeting system, the following points should be made:

1.
2.
3.
4.

Chapter 24, E 5.

1.
2.
3.
4.
5.
6.
7.

Note: The direct labor budget may be prepared before the direct materials purchases budget.

Chapter 24, E 6.

Buchan Manufacturing Company
Sales Budget
For the Year Ended December 31, 20x2

Product Class	January–March	April–June	July–September	October–December	Year
Marine Products					
Mountain Products					
River Products					
Hiking Products					
Running Products					
Biking Products					
Totals					

Chapter 24, E 7.

E-Z Door Company
Production Budget
For the Quarter Ended March 31, 20x7

	January	February	March
Sales in Units			
Add Desired Units of Ending Finished Goods Inventory			
Desired Total Units			
Less Desired Units of Beginning Finished Goods Inventory			
Total Production Units			

Chapter 24, E 8.

E-Z Door Company
Direct Materials Purchases Budget
For the Quarter Ended March 31, 20x7

Number of Units to Be Produced:

	Quantity per Door	Cost per Quantity	Cost per Door	Total Direct Materials Cost
Hinges (in sets)				
Door Panels				
Other Hardware				
Lock				
Handle				
Roller tracks (in sets)				
Rollers				
Total Cost of Direct Materials Purchases				

Chapter 24, E 9.

Henlow Metals Company
Direct Labor Budget
For the Year Ended December 31, 20x1

Cutting Department	Product T	Product M	Product B	Year
Total Production Units				
x Direct Labor Hours per Unit				
Total Direct Labor Hours				
x Direct Labor Cost per Hour				
Total Direct Labor Cost				

Grinding Department	Product T	Product M	Product B	Year
Total Production Units				
x Direct Labor Hours per Unit				
Total Direct Labor Hours				
x Direct Labor Cost per Hour				
Total Direct Labor Cost				
Total Direct Labor Cost				

Chapter 24, E 10.

London Division
Reeds Corporation
Manufacturing Overhead Budget
For the Year Ended December 31, 20x1

Variable Overhead Costs		
Indirect Materials		
Indirect Labor		
Supplies		
Repairs and Maintenance		
Electricity		
Total Variable Overhead		
Fixed Overhead Costs		
Repairs and Maintenance		
Electricity		
Factory Supervision		
Insurance		
Property Taxes		
Depreciation, Machinery		
Depreciation, Building		
Total Fixed Overhead		
Total Manufacturing Overhead Costs		

Chapter 24, E 11.

A cash budget is a projection of the cash receipts and cash payments for a future period. The cash budget serves two purposes:

Car Bros., Inc.
Schedule of Expected Cash Collections from Customers
For the Quarter Ended December 31, 20x1

	Credit Sales	October	November	December	Quarter
Cash Sales					
Collections of Credit Sales:					
August					
September					
October					
November					
December					
Total Cash to Be Collected from Customers					

Chapter 24, P 1.

1. Monthly cost information prepared

							October	November	December
Direct Materials Used									
	Anodized Steel								
		x	2	x	$1.60				
		x		x					
		x		x					
	Leather Strapping								
		x	0.5	x	$4.40				
		x		x					
		x		x					
	Total Direct Materials Used								
Direct Labor Costs									
	Forging Operation								
		x	(	6 min ÷	60 min)	x $12.50			
		x	(	min ÷	min)	x			
		x	(	min ÷	min)	x			
	Leather-Wrapping Operation								
		x	(	min ÷	min)	x			
		x	(	min ÷	min)	x			
		x	(	min ÷	min)	x			
	Total Direct Labor Costs								
Manufacturing Overhead Costs									
	Forging Operation								
		x	70%						
		x							
		x							
	Leather-Wrapping Operation								
		x	50%						
		x							
		x							
	Total Manufacturing Overhead Costs								
Total Manufacturing Costs Budgeted									

Chapter 24, P 1. (Continued)

2. Quarterly budget prepared

Nakamoto Enterprises, Inc.
Cost of Goods Manufactured Budget
For the Quarter Ended December 31, 20x1

	October	November	December	Quarter
Direct Materials Used				
Direct Labor Costs				
Manufacturing Overhead Costs				
Total Manufacturing Costs and Cost of Goods Manufactured				

Chapter 24, P 2.

Operating budgets and budgeted income statement prepared

1. Sales Budget

<table>
<tr><td colspan="6" align="center">Dov's Bath Oils
Sales Budget
For the Year Ended December 31, 20x2</td></tr>
<tr><td></td><td colspan="4" align="center">Quarter</td><td rowspan="2">Year</td></tr>
<tr><td></td><td>1</td><td>2</td><td>3</td><td>4</td></tr>
<tr><td>Sales in Units</td><td></td><td></td><td></td><td></td><td></td></tr>
<tr><td> x Selling Price per Unit</td><td></td><td></td><td></td><td></td><td></td></tr>
<tr><td>Total Sales</td><td></td><td></td><td></td><td></td><td></td></tr>
</table>

2. Production Budget

<table>
<tr><td colspan="6" align="center">Dov's Bath Oils
Production Budget
For the Year Ended December 31, 20x2</td></tr>
<tr><td></td><td colspan="4" align="center">Quarter</td><td rowspan="2">Year</td></tr>
<tr><td></td><td>1</td><td>2</td><td>3</td><td>4</td></tr>
<tr><td>Sales in Units (Budget 1)</td><td></td><td></td><td></td><td></td><td></td></tr>
<tr><td>Add Desired Units of Ending
  Finished Goods Inventory</td><td></td><td></td><td></td><td></td><td></td></tr>
<tr><td>Desired Total Units</td><td></td><td></td><td></td><td></td><td></td></tr>
<tr><td>Less Desired Units of Beginning
  Finished Goods Inventory</td><td></td><td></td><td></td><td></td><td></td></tr>
<tr><td>Total Production Units</td><td></td><td></td><td></td><td></td><td></td></tr>
<tr><td colspan="6">Note 1: Desired units of ending finished goods inventory = 10% of *next* quarter's budgeted sales.</td></tr>
<tr><td colspan="6">Note 2: Desired units of beginning finished goods inventory = 10% of *current* quarter's budgeted sales.</td></tr>
</table>

Chapter 24, P 2. (Continued)

3. Direct Materials Purchases Budget

Dov's Bath Oils
Direct Materials Purchases Budget
For the Year Ended December 31, 20x2

	Quarter 1	Quarter 2	Quarter 3	Quarter 4	Year
Total Production Units (Budget 2)					
x 3 Ounces per Unit					
Total Production Needs in Ounces					
Add Desired Ounces of Ending Direct Materials Inventory					
Less Desired Ounces of Beginning Direct Materials Inventory					
Total Ounces of Direct Materials to Be Purchased					
x Cost per Ounce					
Total Cost of Direct Materials Purchases					

Note 1: Desired ounces of ending direct materials inventory = 20% of *next* quarter's budgeted production needs in ounces.

Note 2: Desired ounces of beginning direct materials inventory = 20% of *current* quarter's budgeted production needs in ounces.

Note 3: Assume that budgeted production needs in ounces for the first quarter of 20x3 = 18,000 ounces.

4. Direct Labor Budget

Dov's Bath Oils
Direct Labor Budget
For the Year Ended December 31, 20x2

	Quarter 1	Quarter 2	Quarter 3	Quarter 4	Year
Total Production Units (Budget 2)					
x Direct Labor Hours per Unit					
Total Direct Labor Hours					
x Direct Labor Cost per Hour					
Total Direct Labor Cost					

Chapter 24, P 2. (Continued)

5. Manufacturing Overhead Budget

Dov's Bath Oils
Manufacturing Overhead Budget
For the Year Ended December 31, 20x2

	Quarter 1	Quarter 2	Quarter 3	Quarter 4	Year
Variable Overhead Costs					
Factory Supplies					
Employee Benefits					
Inspection					
Maintenance and Repair					
Utilities					
Total Variable Overhead					
Fixed Overhead Costs					
Depreciation, Machinery					
Depreciation, Building					
Supervision					
Maintenance and Repair					
Other Overhead Expenses					
Total Fixed Overhead					
Total Manufacturing Overhead Costs					

Predetermined overhead rate = _____ ÷ _____ direct labor hours = _____ per direct labor hour

Chapter 24, P 2. (Continued)

6. Selling and Administrative Expense Budget

Dov's Bath Oils
Selling and Administrative Expense Budget
For the Year Ended December 31, 20x2

	Quarter 1	Quarter 2	Quarter 3	Quarter 4	Year
Variable Selling and Administrative Expenses					
Delivery Expenses					
Sales Commissions					
Accounting					
Other Administrative Expenses					
Total Variable Selling and Administrative Expenses					
Fixed Selling and Administrative Expenses					
Sales Salaries					
Depreciation, Office Equipment					
Taxes and Insurance					
Total Fixed Selling and Administrative Expenses					
Total Selling and Administrative Expenses					

Chapter 24, P 2. (Continued)

7. Cost of Goods Manufactured Budget

Dov's Bath Oils
Cost of Goods Manufactured Budget
For the Year Ended December 31, 20x2

Direct Materials Used				
Materials Inventory, December 31, 20x1				
Purchases for 20x2				Budget 3
Cost of Materials Available for Use				
Less Materials Inventory,				
December 31, 20x2				
Cost of Direct Materials Used				
Direct Labor Costs				Budget 4
Manufacturing Overhead Costs				Budget 5
Total Manufacturing Costs				
Work in Process Inventory, December 31, 20x1				
Less Work in Process Inventory,				
December 31, 20x2*				
Cost of Goods Manufactured				
Manufactured cost per unit =	÷		units	=

*It is a company policy to have no units in process at year end.

Chapter 24, P 2. (Continued)

8. Budgeted Income Statement

Dov's Bath Oils
Budgeted Income Statement
For the Year Ended December 31, 20x2

Sales				
Cost of Goods Sold				
Finished Goods Inventory, December 31, 20x1*				
Cost of Goods Manufactured				Budget 7
Cost of Goods Available for Sale				
Less Finished Goods Inventory, December 31, 20x2*				
Cost of Goods Sold				
Gross Margin				
Selling and Administrative Expenses				Budget 6
Income from Operations				
Income Taxes Expense ( )				**
Net Income				

*Assumes a constant product unit cost during the year.

December 31, 20x1		December 31, 20x2		
	units		units	(Part 2)
x		x		(Part 7)

**Rounded.

Chapter 24, P 3.

Cash receipts from sales on account computed

Month	Credit Sales	January	February	March
November				
December				
January				
February				
March				
Totals				

1. **Cash budget prepared**

Woodhull Nurseries, Inc.
Monthly Cash Budgets—Southern Division
For the Quarter Ended March 31, 20x2

	January	February	March	Quarter
Cash Receipts				
Cash Sales				
Credit Sales				
Total Cash Receipts				
Cash Payments				
Purchases				
Salaries and Wages				
Utilities				
Collection Fees				
Rent				
Supplies				
Small Tools				
Miscellaneous				
Total Cash Payments				
Cash Increase (Decrease)				
Beginning Cash Balance				
Ending Cash Balance				

2. **Loan possibility discussed**

Chapter 24, P 4.

Preliminary schedules:				
	Materials Inventory			
		Beginning Balance		
		Direct materials purchases		
		Direct materials available for use		
		Less direct materials used		
		Ending balance		
	Work in Process Inventory			
		Beginning balance		
		Added during period:		
			Direct materials used	
			Direct labor	
			Manufacturing overhead	
		Total costs in production		
		Less cost of goods manufactured		
		Ending balance		
	Finished Goods Inventory			
		Beginning balance		
		Cost of goods manufactured		
		Cost of goods available for sale		
		Less cost of goods sold		
		Ending balance		

Chapter 24, P 4. (Continued)

1. Budgeted income statement prepared

Beyond Video Company, Inc.
Budgeted Income Statement
For the Quarter Ended March 31, 20x1

Sales		
Less Cost of Goods Sold		
Gross Margin		
Operating Expenses		
Selling Expenses		
General and Administrative Expenses		
Total Operating Expenses		
Income from Operations		
Interest Expense		
Income Before Income Taxes		
Income Taxes Expense ( )		
Net Income		

Chapter 24, P 4. (Continued)

2. Budgeted balance sheet prepared

Beyond Video Company, Inc.
Budgeted Balance Sheet
March 31, 20x1

Assets

Current Assets
- Cash
- Accounts Receivable (___ x ___)
- Materials Inventory
- Work in Process Inventory
- Finished Goods Inventory
- Prepaid Expenses
- Total Current Assets

Plant and Equipment
- Less Accumulated Depreciation *

Other Assets

Total Assets

Liabilities

Current Liabilities
- Accounts Payable
- Income Taxes Payable
- Total Current Liabilities

Mortgage Payable (___ − ___)

Total Liabilities

Stockholders' Equity

Common Stock

Retained Earnings
- Beginning Balance
- Net Income for Period
- Retained Earnings, March 31, 20x1

Total Stockholders' Equity

Total Liabilities and Stockholders' Equity

*Accumulated depreciation = ___ + (___ × 0.05 ÷ ___) =

Chapter 24, P 5.

Thomas's Wellness Centers, Inc.
Cash Budget
For the Quarter Ended March 31, 20x4

Item	January	February	March	Total
Cash Receipts				
Membership Dues				
Medical Examinations				
Aerobics Classes				
High-Protein Food Sales				
Total Cash Receipts				
Cash Payments				
Salaries and Wages				
Corporate Officers				
Medical Doctors				
Nurses				
Clerical Staff				
Aerobics Instructors				
Clinic Staff				
Maintenance Staff				
Health Food Servers				
Purchases				
Muscle-Toning Machines				
Pool Supplies				
Health Food				
Medical Supplies				
Medical Clothing				
Medical Equipment				
Advertising				
Utilities Expense				
Insurance				
Fire				
Liability				
Property Taxes				
Federal Income Taxes				
Miscellaneous				
Total Payments				
Cash Increase (Decrease)				
Beginning Cash Balance				
Ending Cash Balance				

Copyright © Houghton Mifflin Company. All rights reserved.

Chapter 24, P 6.

1. 20x5 budgeted income statement prepared

Walker House, Inc.
Budgeted Income Statement
For the Year Ended December 31, 20x5

Net Receipts			
Operating Expenses			
Salaries			
Staging			
Executive			
Travel Costs			
Auctioneer Services			
Space Rental Costs			
Printing Costs			
Advertising Expense			
Insurance			
Merchandise			
Liability			
Home Office Costs			
Shipping Costs			
Miscellaneous			
Total Operating Expenses			
Income from Operations			
Income Taxes Expense ( )			
Net Income			

2. Trend in company's operations discussed

Chapter 24, P 7.

Computation of cash receipts from credit sales:

Month	Total Credit Sales x Collection %			Cash Receipts on Account July	August	September
May	(	x	0.20)			
June	(	x	)			
	(	x	)			
July	(	x	)			
	(	x	)			
	(	x	)			
August	(	x	)			
	(	x	)			
September	(	x	)			
Totals						

Chapter 24, P 7. (Continued)

1. **Cash budget prepared**

Market Produce, Inc.
Monthly Cash Budgets
For the Quarter Ended September 30, 20x3

	July	August	September	Quarter
Cash Receipts				
Cash Sales				
Credit Sales				
Total Cash Receipts				
Cash Payments				
Produce Purchases				
Salaries and Wages				
Heat, Light, and Power				
Bank Collection Fees				
Rent				
Supplies				
Equipment Repairs				
Miscellaneous				
Total Cash Payments				
Cash Increase (Decrease)				
Beginning Cash Balance				
Ending Cash Balance				

2. **Loan possibility discussed**

Chapter 24, P 8.

Preliminary schedules:

- **Materials Inventory**
  - Beginning balance
  - Direct materials purchases
  - Direct materials available for use
  - Less direct materials used
  - Ending balance
- **Work in Process Inventory**
  - Beginning balance
  - Added during period:
    - Direct materials used
    - Direct labor
    - Manufacturing overhead
  - Total costs in production
  - Less cost of goods manufactured
  - Ending balance
- **Finished Goods Inventory**
  - Beginning balance
  - Cost of goods manufactured
  - Cost of goods available for sale
  - Less cost of goods sold
  - Ending balance

Chapter 24, P 8. (Continued)

1. Budgeted income statement prepared

Runnymeade Products, Inc. Budgeted Income Statement For the Quarter Ended June 30, 20x1	
Sales	
Less Cost of Goods Sold	
Gross Margin	
Selling and Administrative Expenses	
Income from Operations	
Interest Expense	
Income Before Income Taxes	
Income Taxes Expense ( )	
Projected Net Income	

Chapter 24, P 8. (Continued)

2. Budgeted balance sheet prepared

<table>
<tr><td colspan="3">Runnymeade Products, Inc.
Budgeted Balance Sheet
June 30, 20x1</td></tr>
<tr><td colspan="3">Assets</td></tr>
<tr><td colspan="3">Current Assets</td></tr>
<tr><td>Cash</td><td></td><td></td></tr>
<tr><td>Accounts Receivable</td><td></td><td></td></tr>
<tr><td>Materials Inventory</td><td></td><td></td></tr>
<tr><td>Work in Process Inventory</td><td></td><td></td></tr>
<tr><td>Finished Goods Inventory</td><td></td><td></td></tr>
<tr><td>Prepaid Expenses</td><td></td><td></td></tr>
<tr><td>Total Current Assets</td><td></td><td></td></tr>
<tr><td colspan="3">Plant, Furniture, and Fixtures</td></tr>
<tr><td>Less Accumulated Depreciation</td><td></td><td></td></tr>
<tr><td colspan="3">Other Assets</td></tr>
<tr><td>Patents</td><td></td><td></td></tr>
<tr><td colspan="3">Total Assets</td></tr>
<tr><td colspan="3">Liabilities</td></tr>
<tr><td colspan="3">Current Liabilities</td></tr>
<tr><td>Accounts Payable</td><td></td><td></td></tr>
<tr><td>Income Taxes Payable</td><td></td><td></td></tr>
<tr><td>Total Current Liabilities</td><td></td><td></td></tr>
<tr><td colspan="3">Long-Term Liabilities</td></tr>
<tr><td>Notes Payable (–   )</td><td></td><td></td></tr>
<tr><td colspan="3">Total Liabilities</td></tr>
<tr><td colspan="3">Stockholders' Equity</td></tr>
<tr><td colspan="3">Common Stock</td></tr>
<tr><td colspan="3">Retained Earnings</td></tr>
<tr><td>Beginning Balance</td><td></td><td></td></tr>
<tr><td>Net Income for Period</td><td></td><td></td></tr>
<tr><td>Retained Earnings,
June 30, 20x1</td><td></td><td></td></tr>
<tr><td colspan="3">Total Stockholders' Equity</td></tr>
<tr><td colspan="3">Total Liabilities and Stockholders' Equity</td></tr>
<tr><td colspan="3">Note: No dividends were paid.</td></tr>
</table>

Chapter 24, SD 4.

Budget for Cookie Sales at Fall Football Games

	Game 1	Game 2	Game 3	Game 4	Game 5	Totals
Revenues:						
Cookie Sales						
Less Sales Commission						
Net Revenues						
Costs:						
Cost of Cookies*						
Packaging						
Tools and Supplies						
Advertising						
Kitchen Fee						
Cleanup						
Total Costs						
Projected Income						

*Projections based on students' research.

Chapter 24, SD 5.

1. Budgeted income statement revised

Squizzero Enterprises
Motor Division
Revised Budgeted Income Statement
For the Years Ended December 31, 20x4 and 20x5

Account	Budget—12/31/x4 Amount	Percent of Sales	Budget—12/31/x5 Amount	Percent of Sales
Net Sales				
Radios				
Appliances				
Telephones				
Miscellaneous				
Net Sales				
Less Cost of Goods Sold				
Gross Margin				
Operating Expenses				
Wages				
Warehouse				
Purchasing				
Delivery/Shipping				
Maintenance				
Salaries				
Supervisory				
Executive				
Purchases, Supplies				
Merchandise Moving Equipment				
Maintenance				
Depreciation				
Building Rent				
Sales Commissions				
Insurance				
Fire				
Liability				
Utilities				
Taxes				
Property				
Payroll				
Miscellaneous				
Total Operating Expenses				
Income from Operations				

Chapter 24, SD 5. (Continued)

2. The following points should be brought to the attention of the Motor Division's managers:

   a.

   b.

   c.

   d.

   e.

   f.

Chapter 24, MRA 4.

1. Operating budgets and budgeted income statement prepared

1. Sales Budget

Hi-Flyer Company
Sales Budget
For the Year Ended December 31, 20x1

	Quarter 1	Quarter 2	Quarter 3	Quarter 4	Year
Sales in Units					
x Selling Price per Unit					
Total Sales					

2. Production Budget

Hi-Flyer Company
Production Budget
For the Year Ended December 31, 20x1

	Quarter 1	Quarter 2	Quarter 3	Quarter 4	Year
Sales in Units (Budget 1)					
Add Desired Units of Ending Finished Goods Inventory					
Desired Total Units					
Less Desired Units of Beginning Finished Goods Inventory					
Total Production Units					

Note 1: Desired units of ending finished goods inventory = 10% of *next* quarter's budgeted sales.
Note 2: Desired units of beginning finished goods inventory = 1,000 units.
Note 3: Assume that budgeted sales for the first quarter of 20x2 = 15,000 units.

Chapter 24, MRA 4. (Continued)

3. Direct Materials Purchases Budget

Hi-Flyer Company
Direct Materials Purchases Budget
For the Year Ended December 31, 20x1

	Quarter 1	Quarter 2	Quarter 3	Quarter 4	Year
Total Production Units (Budget 2)					
x 10 Ounces per Unit					
Total Production Needs in Ounces					
Add Desired Ounces of Ending Direct Materials Inventory					
Less Desired Ounces of Beginning Direct Materials Inventory					
Total Ounces of Direct Materials to Be Purchased					
x Cost per Ounce					
Total Cost of Direct Materials Purchases					

Note 1: Desired ounces of ending direct materials inventory = 20% of *next* quarter's budgeted production needs in ounces.
Note 2: Desired ounces of beginning direct materials inventory = 20% of *current* quarter's budgeted production needs in ounces.
Note 3: Assume that budgeted production needs in ounces for the first quarter of 20x2 = 150,000 ounces.
Note 4: The desired direct materials inventory balance at December 31, 20x0 = 34,000 ounces x $.05 per ounce = $1,700 and at December 31, 20x1 = 30,000 ounces x $.05 per ounce = $1,500.

4. Direct Labor Budget

Hi-Flyer Company
Direct Labor Budget
For the Year Ended December 31, 20x1

	Quarter 1	Quarter 2	Quarter 3	Quarter 4	Year
Total Production Units (Budget 2)					
x Direct Labor Hours per Unit					
Total Direct Labor Hours					
x Direct Labor Cost per Hour					
Total Direct Labor Cost					

Chapter 24, MRA 4. (Continued)

5. Manufacturing Overhead Budget

Hi-Flyer Company
Manufacturing Overhead Budget
For the Year Ended December 31, 20x1

	Variable Rates	Quarter 1	Quarter 2	Quarter 3	Quarter 4	Year
Variable Overhead Costs						
Indirect Materials	0.18					
Employee Benefits						
Inspection						
Maintenance and Repair						
Utilities						
Total Variable Overhead						
Fixed Overhead Costs						
Depreciation, Machinery						
Depreciation, Building						
Supervision						
Maintenance and Repair						
Other Overhead Expenses						
Total Fixed Overhead						
Total Manufacturing Overhead Costs						

Predetermined Overhead Rate = _____ ÷ _____ direct labor hours = _____ per direct labor hour

Chapter 24, MRA 4. (Continued)

6. Selling and Administrative Expense Budget

Hi-Flyer Company
Selling and Administrative Expense Budget
For the Year Ended December 31, 20x1

	Quarter 1	Quarter 2	Quarter 3	Quarter 4	Year
Variable Selling and Administrative Expenses					
Delivery Expenses					
Sales Commissions					
Accounting					
Other Administrative Expenses					
Total Variable Selling and Administrative Expenses					
Fixed Selling and Administrative Expenses					
Sales Salaries					
Executive Salaries					
Depreciation, Office Equipment					
Taxes and Insurance					
Total Fixed Selling and Administrative Expenses					
Total Selling and Administrative Expenses					

Chapter 24, MRA 4. (Continued)

7. Cost of Goods Manufactured Budget

Hi-Flyer Company
Cost of Goods Manufactured Budget
For the Year Ended December 31, 20x1

			Sources of Data
Direct Materials Used			
Materials Inventory, December 31, 20x0			Budget 3, Note 4
Purchases for 20x1			Budget 3
Cost of Direct Materials Available for Use			
Less Materials Inventory, December 31, 20x1			Budget 3, Note 4
Cost of Direct Materials Used			
Direct Labor Costs			Budget 4
Manufacturing Overhead Costs			Budget 5
Total Manufacturing Costs			
Work in Process Inventory, December 31, 20x0*			
Less Work in Process Inventory,			
December 31, 20x1*			
Cost of Goods Manufactured			
Manufactured cost per unit = ÷ units =			

*It is a company policy to have no units in process at the beginning or end of the year.

Chapter 24, MRA 4. (Continued)

8. Budgeted Income Statement

Hi-Flyer Company
Budgeted Income Statement
For the Year Ended December 31, 20x1

			Sources of Data
Sales			Budget 1
Cost of Goods Sold			
Finished Goods Inventory, December 31, 20x0*			
Cost of Goods Manufactured			Budget 7
Total Cost of Goods Available for Sale			
Less Finished Goods Inventory, December 31, 20x1*			
Cost of Goods Sold			
Gross Margin			
Selling and Administrative Expenses			Budget 6
Income from Operations			
Interest Expense (8% x)			
Income Before Income Taxes			
Income Taxes Expense (30%)			
Net Income			

*Finished Goods Inventory balances assume that product unit costs were the same in 20x0 and 20x1.

December 31, 20x0		December 31, 20x1		
	units		units	Budget 2
x		x		Budget 7

Chapter 24, MRA 4. (Continued)

2. Change in income from operations discussed

Change in income from operations:	
Income from operations from Budget 8	
Less income from operations from Exhibit 8 (in text)	
Change in income from operations	

Check:

Increase in sales

($5 x _____ units)

Increase in direct materials costs

($0.05 x _____ ounces x _____ units)

Increase in direct labor costs

($6 x _____ direct labor hour per unit x _____ units)

Increase in variable overhead costs

(_____ – _____)

Increase in delivery expenses

(_____ per unit x _____ units)

Increase in variable selling and administrative expenses (except delivery)

(_____ per unit x _____ units)

Increase in income from operations

Note: The difference in the two calculations stems from the rounding of the product cost per unit.

Chapter 25, SE 1.

Chapter 25, SE 2.

Standard costs provide the following advantages to management:

1.
2.
3.
4.
5.
6.

Chapter 25, SE 3.

Direct materials cost					
(		x	5 lbs.	)	
Direct labor cost					
(		x	0.4 hr.	)	
Variable manufacturing overhead					
(		x		machine hrs.)	
Fixed manufacturing overhead					
(		x		machine hrs.)	
Total standard unit cost					

Chapter 25, SE 4.

The tolerance in the exercise is ±5 percent. The following percentages need to be calculated:

Product 4	( )
Product 6	( )
Product 7	( )
Product 9	( )
Product 12	( )

Chapter 25, SE 4. (Continued)

Possible causes of variances:

Product 6

Product 7

Chapter 25, SE 5.

Direct Materials Price Variance	= (Standard Price − Actual Price) × Actual Quantity
	= (−) × pounds
	= ( ) × pounds = ( )

Direct Materials Quantity Variance	= Standard Price × (Standard Quantity − Actual Quantity)
	= × [(× pounds) − pounds]
	= × (pounds − pounds) =

Chapter 25, SE 6.

Direct Labor Rate Variance	= (Standard Rate − Actual Rate) × Actual Hours
	= [− (÷ hours)] × hours
	= (−) × hours
	= ( ) × hours = ( )

Direct Labor Efficiency Variance	= Standard Rate × (Standard Hours Allowed − Actual Hours)
	= × [(× 0.4 hour) − hours]
	= × (hours − hours)
	= × ( ) = ( )

Chapter 25, SE 7.

Cost Category	Units Produced 10,000	12,000	14,000	Variable Cost per Unit
Direct materials				
Direct labor				
Variable manufacturing overhead				
Total variable costs				
Fixed manufacturing overhead				
Total costs				

Chapter 25, SE 8.

Controllable manufacturing overhead variance:			
Budgeted manufacturing overhead for _____ machine hours allowed			
(_____ good units x _____ machine hours per unit)			
Variable manufacturing overhead costs (_____ per machine hour x _____ machine hours)			
Budgeted fixed manufacturing overhead cost			
Total budgeted manufacturing overhead			
Less actual manufacturing overhead costs incurred			
Variable			
Fixed			
Controllable manufacturing overhead variance			( )
Manufacturing overhead volume variance:			
Standard manufacturing overhead applied			
[(_____ / machine hour + _____ / machine hour) x _____ machine hours]			
Less total budgeted manufacturing overhead (see computation above)			
Manufacturing overhead volume variance			( )

Chapter 25, SE 9.

Chapter 25, E 1.

To:
From:
Date:
Subject:

Chapter 25, E 2.

Computation of new direct materials standards:

Direct materials quantity standard

		sq. yds. ÷		units =		sq. yds. per unit

Direct materials price standard

		÷		sq. yds. =		per sq. yd.

Computation of new direct labor standards:

Direct labor time standards

Machine H:		hours ÷		units
	=	direct labor hours per unit		
Machine K:		hours ÷		units
	=	direct labor hours per unit		

Direct labor rate standards

Machine H:		per hour	x	110%	=		per hour
Machine K:		per hour	x		=		per hour

Chapter 25, E 3.

Standard unit cost:

Direct materials costs

    Electronic components

		per set	x		set

    Heavy-duty canvas

		per sq. meter	x		sq. meters

Direct labor costs

    Electronics Department

		per hour	x		hours

    Assembly Department

		per hour	x		hours

Manufacturing overhead

    Variable manufacturing overhead

		per direct labor hour	x		hours

    Fixed manufacturing overhead

		per direct labor hour	x		hours

Total standard unit cost

Chapter 25, E 4.

Computation of direct materials price variance:

Standard direct materials price					
Less actual direct materials price					
Difference in price					( )
Direct Materials Price Variance	=	(Standard Price − Actual Price) × Actual Quantity			
	=	( ) × (	sq. yds. ×	90)	
	=	( )			

Computation of direct materials quantity variance:

Standard quantity	(8.0 sq. yds. ×)	sq. yds.
Less actual quantity	(sq. yds. ×)	sq. yds.
Difference in quantity		sq. yds. ( )
Direct Materials Quantity Variance	= Standard Price × (Standard Quantity − Actual Quantity)	
	= × sq. yds. ( )	
	= ( )	

Chapter 25, E 5.

1. Direct labor rate variance computed

Standard direct labor rate			
Less actual direct labor rate			
(÷ hrs.)			
Difference in labor rate		( )	

Direct Labor Rate Variance	= (Standard Rate − Actual Rate) × Actual Hours
	= ( ) × hrs.
	= ( )

2. Direct labor efficiency variance computed

Standard direct labor hours allowed		
(engine blocks × hrs./block)	hrs.	
Less actual direct labor hours worked	hrs.	
Difference in direct labor hours	hrs. ( )	

Direct Labor Efficiency Variance	= Standard Rate × (Standard Hours Allowed − Actual Hours)
	= × hrs. ( )
	= ( )
Total variance	= ( ) + ( ) = ( )

Chapter 25, E 6.

Helms Company
Flexible Budget
For the Year Ended December 31, 20x5

Cost Category	Units Produced 18,000	Units Produced 20,000	Units Produced 22,000	Variable Cost per Unit
Direct materials				
Direct labor				
Variable manufacturing overhead				
Operating supplies				
Indirect labor				
Other				
Total variable costs				
Fixed manufacturing overhead				
Depreciation				
Supervisory salaries				
Property taxes and insurance				
Other				
Total fixed manufacturing overhead				
Total costs				

Flexible budget formula for 20x5:

Total Budgeted Costs = (_____ x Units Produced) + _____

Chapter 25, E 7.

Standard manufacturing overhead costs applied							
	to good units produced	[	$4.75	* per direct labor hour			
	x (		clamming buckets	x 0.2	direct labor		
	hour per clamming bucket)]						
Less actual manufacturing overhead costs incurred							
Total manufacturing overhead variance							( )
Controllable manufacturing overhead variance							
	Budgeted manufacturing overhead for	10,100					
	clamming buckets:						
		Variable manufacturing overhead cost					
		[	per direct labor hour	x (			
	clamming buckets	x		direct labor hour per			
	clamming bucket)]						
		Budgeted fixed manufacturing overhead cost					
		Total budgeted manufacturing overhead					
	Less actual manufacturing overhead costs incurred						
	Controllable manufacturing overhead variance						( )
Manufacturing overhead volume variance							
	Standard manufacturing overhead applied						
	[	$4.75	* per direct labor hour	x (			
	clamming buckets	x		direct labor hour per			
	clamming bucket)]						
	Less total budgeted manufacturing overhead (see above)						
	Manufacturing overhead volume variance						( )
Check:	Controllable manufacturing overhead variance						( )
	Manufacturing overhead volume variance						( )
	Total manufacturing overhead variance						( )
*	The		standard fixed manufacturing overhead rate was computed as follows:				
		budgeted fixed manufacturing overhead	÷		hours (normal capacity)		
	=		per hour				
		of variable manufacturing overhead	+		of fixed overhead		
	=		per direct labor hour				

Chapter 25, E 8.

1. Under- or overapplied manufacturing overhead for December computed

Fixed Manufacturing Overhead Rate	=	Budgeted Fixed Costs ÷ Normal Capacity in Machine Hours			
	=	÷		machine hours	
	=		per machine hour		
Total Manufacturing Overhead Applied	=	(Variable Manufacturing Overhead Rate + Fixed Manufacturing Overhead Rate) × Standard Hours Allowed			
	=	(+) ×		hours	
	=				

Overapplied manufacturing overhead			
Manufacturing overhead applied			
Actual manufacturing overhead incurred		*	
Overapplied manufacturing overhead			
* variable + fixed.			

2. Manufacturing overhead variances computed

Controllable manufacturing overhead variance			
Budgeted manufacturing overhead			
(flexible budget) for standard hours allowed:			
Variable manufacturing overhead rate × standard			
hours allowed (× hours)			
Budgeted fixed manufacturing overhead			
Less actual manufacturing overhead incurred			
(from above)			
Controllable manufacturing overhead variance			( )
Manufacturing overhead volume variance			
Standard manufacturing overhead applied			
Total manufacturing overhead rate × standard hours			
allowed (× hours)			
Less total budgeted manufacturing overhead (flexible			
budget) for standard hours allowed (from above)			
Manufacturing overhead volume variance			( )
Check Controllable manufacturing overhead variance			( )
Manufacturing overhead volume variance			( )
Total manufacturing overhead variance			( )

Chapter 25, E 9.

Jim La Plante must identify the causes of the unfavorable direct labor efficiency variance for the roof structure work on the Bogs Apartment Complex. He should ask the manager of the roof structure work for the following information:

Chapter 25, P 1.

1. Total standard cost of direct materials for 20x1 computed
2. Total standard unit cost for 20x1 computed

Direct materials costs						
Wood framing materials						
Deluxe front door						
Door hardware						
Exterior siding						
Electrical materials						
Interior finishing materials						
Total cost of direct materials						
Direct labor costs						
Carpenter	(	per hour	x	hours)		
Door specialist	(	per hour	x	hours)		
Electrician	(	per hour	x	hours)		
Total cost of direct labor						
Manufacturing overhead						
40% of cost of direct materials	(		x	)		
Total standard unit cost of front entrance						

3. Total standard unit cost for 20x2 computed

Direct materials						
Wood framing materials:		x				
Deluxe front door						
Door hardware	(	x	)			
Exterior siding	(	−	)			
Electrical materials	(	x	)			
Interior finishing materials						
Total cost of direct materials						
Direct labor						
Carpenter	(	per hour	x	hours)		
Door specialist	(	per hour	x	hours)		
Electrician	(	per hour	x	hours)		
Total cost of direct labor						
Manufacturing overhead						
25% of cost of direct materials	(		x	)		
Total standard unit cost of front entrance						

Chapter 25, P 2.

1. Direct materials price and quantity variances computed

	Liquid Plastic	Additive
Standard cost		
Standard price x standard quantity		
[____ per gram x (____ baskets x ____ gram per basket)]		
[____ per gram x (____ baskets x ____ gram per basket)]		
Less actual cost		
Actual cost x actual quantity		
____ per gram x ____ grams		
____ per gram x ____ grams		
Total direct materials cost variance	( )	( )
Direct materials price variance		
Standard price		
Less actual price (____ ÷ ____);		
(____ ÷ ____)		
Difference in price	( )	( )
Direct materials price variance—liquid plastic		
= difference in price x actual quantity		
= ( ) x ____ grams		
= ( )		
Direct materials price variance—additive		
= ( ) x ____ grams		
= ( )		

Chapter 25, P 2. (Continued)

	Liquid Plastic	Additive
Direct materials quantity variance		
Standard total quantity		**
Less actual total quantity		
Difference in quantity	( )	( )
Direct materials quantity variance—Liquid Plastic		
= per gram x ( ) grams		
= ( )		
Direct materials quantity variance—Additive		
= per gram x ( ) grams		
= ( )		

	Liquid Plastic	Additive
Check:		
Direct materials price variance	( )	( )
Direct materials quantity variance	( )	( )
Total direct materials cost variance	( )	( )
* x 0.8 gram per basket		
** x gram per basket		

Chapter 25, P 2. (Continued)

2. Direct labor rate and efficiency variances computed

	Molding	Trimming/Packing
Standard cost		
Standard rate x standard hours allowed		
per hour x (÷ 100) x hour		
per hour x (÷) x hours		
Less actual cost		
Actual rate x actual hours		
per hour x hours		
per hour x hours		
Total direct labor cost variance	( )	( )

	Molding	Trimming/Packing
Direct labor rate variance		
Standard rate		
Less actual rate		
Difference in rate	( )	( )
Direct labor rate variance—Molding		
= difference in rate x actual hours		
= ( ) x hours		
= ( )		
Direct labor rate variance—Trimming/Packing		
= ( ) x hours		
= ( )		

Chapter 25, P 2. (Continued)

	Molding	Trimming/Packing
Direct labor efficiency variance		
Standard hours allowed*		
Less actual hours		
Difference in hours		( )

Direct labor efficiency variance—Molding
=	Standard rate x difference in hours
=	per hour x
=	

Direct labor efficiency variance—Trimming/Packing
=	per hour x ( )
=	( )

	Molding	Trimming/Packing
Check:		
Rate variance	( )	( )
Efficiency variance		( )
Total direct labor cost variance	( )	( )
*	x	for molding;
	x	for trimming/packing

Chapter 25, P 3.

1. Flexible budget prepared

Maltese Home Products Company
Cottonwood Division
Monthly Flexible Budget

Cost Category	Units Produced 45,000	50,000	55,000	Variable Cost per Unit
Direct materials				
Direct labor				
Variable manufacturing overhead				
Indirect labor				
Supplies				
Heat and power				
Other				
Total variable costs				
Fixed manufacturing overhead				
Heat and power				
Depreciation				
Insurance and taxes				
Other				
Total fixed manufacturing overhead costs				
Total costs				

2. Flexible budget formula developed

Total Budgeted Costs = (x   Units Produced) +

Chapter 25, P 3. (Continued)

3. Revised performance report prepared

<table>
<tr><td colspan="4" align="center">**Maltese Home Products Company**
Cottonwood Division
Performance Report
For April 20x4</td></tr>
<tr><td>**Cost Category**
(Variable Unit Cost)</td><td>**Budget***</td><td>**Actual Cost**</td><td>**Difference
Under (Over)
Budget**</td></tr>
<tr><td>Direct materials (   )</td><td></td><td></td><td></td></tr>
<tr><td>Direct labor (   )</td><td></td><td></td><td></td></tr>
<tr><td>Manufacturing overhead</td><td></td><td></td><td></td></tr>
<tr><td>   variable</td><td></td><td></td><td></td></tr>
<tr><td>   Indirect labor (   )</td><td></td><td></td><td></td></tr>
<tr><td>   Supplies (   )</td><td></td><td></td><td></td></tr>
<tr><td>   Heat and power (   )</td><td></td><td></td><td></td></tr>
<tr><td>   Other (   )</td><td></td><td></td><td></td></tr>
<tr><td>Total variable costs</td><td></td><td></td><td></td></tr>
<tr><td>Fixed</td><td></td><td></td><td></td></tr>
<tr><td>   Heat and power</td><td></td><td></td><td></td></tr>
<tr><td>   Depreciation</td><td></td><td></td><td></td></tr>
<tr><td>   Insurance and taxes</td><td></td><td></td><td></td></tr>
<tr><td>   Other</td><td></td><td></td><td></td></tr>
<tr><td>Total fixed costs</td><td></td><td></td><td></td></tr>
<tr><td>Total costs</td><td></td><td></td><td></td></tr>
<tr><td colspan="4">* Based on actual production of _____ units.</td></tr>
</table>

4. Performance reports compared

Chapter 25, P 4.

1. Variances computed

Total direct materials variance

    Standard direct materials cost

        Standard price x standard quantity

            per meter x (mats x   meter per mat)

    Less actual direct materials cost

        Actual price x actual quantity

            * per meter x   meters

Total direct materials cost variance   ( )

  *   ÷   meters

a. Direct materials price variance

    Standard direct materials price

    Less actual direct materials price

    Difference in price   ( )

    Direct Materials Price Variance = (Standard Price − Actual Price) x Actual Quantity

            = ( ) x   meters

            = ( )

b. Direct materials quantity variance

    Standard direct materials quantity

    (x   meter per mat)   meters

    Less actual direct materials quantity   meters

    Difference in quantity   ( )

    Direct Materials Quantity Variance = Standard Price x (Standard Quantity − Actual Quantity)

            per meter x ( )

            = ( )

    Check:

        Direct materials price variance   ( )

        Direct materials quantity variance   ( )

        Total direct materials cost variance   ( )

Chapter 25, P 4. (Continued)

Total direct labor variance					
	Standard direct labor cost				
		Standard rate x standard hours allowed			
			per hour x (	mats x	hour per mat)	
	Less actual direct labor cost				
		Actual rate x actual hours			
			per hour x	hours		
Total direct labor cost variance					( )

c. Direct labor rate variance

Standard direct labor rate		per hour
Less actual direct labor rate		
(÷)		per hour
Difference in rate		( )
Direct Labor Rate Variance	= (Standard Rate − Actual Rate) x Actual Hours	
	= ( ) x hours	
	= ( )	

d. Direct labor efficiency variance

Standard direct labor hours allowed		
(x hour)		hours
Less actual direct labor hours		hours
Difference in hours		( )
Direct Labor Efficiency Variance	= Standard Rate x (Standard Hours Allowed − Actual Hours)	
	= per hour x hours ( )	
	= ( )	
Check:		
Direct labor rate variance		( )
Direct labor efficiency variance		( )
Total direct labor cost variance		( )

Chapter 25, P 4. (Continued)

Total manufacturing overhead variance										
	Standard manufacturing overhead costs applied to									
	good units produced									
		(Variable + fixed manufacturing overhead rates)								
		x (good units produced x standard hours per unit)								
		(		+	0.8	) x (		hours	x 0.2	
	hour per mat)									
	Less actual manufacturing overhead costs incurred									
Total manufacturing overhead variance									( )	

e. Controllable manufacturing overhead variance computed

Budgeted manufacturing overhead (flexible budget)							
	Variable manufacturing overhead cost						
	$1.50 x (		hours x		)		
	Budgeted fixed manufacturing overhead cost						
	Total budgeted manufacturing overhead						
Less actual manufacturing overhead costs incurred							
Controllable manufacturing overhead variance						( )	

f. Manufacturing overhead volume variance computed

Standard manufacturing overhead applied						
	per hour x (		hours	x		
hour per mat)						
Less total budgeted manufacturing overhead (see part e)						
Manufacturing overhead volume variance					( )	
Check:						
	Controllable manufacturing overhead variance					( )
	Manufacturing overhead volume variance					( )
	Total manufacturing overhead cost variance					( )

Chapter 25, P 4. (Continued)

2. Performance report prepared

Ezekiel Rug Company
Production Performance and Cost Variance Report
Product: All-Vinyl Doormats
For the Month of August 20x5

Productivity Summary

| Normal capacity | _____ units |
| Good units produced | _____ units |

Cost and Variance Analysis

	Standard Cost	Actual Cost Incurred	Total Variance	Variance Breakdown Type	Amount
Direct materials			( )	Direct materials price variance	( )
					( )
Direct labor			( )		( )
					( )
Manufacturing overhead			( )		( )
					( )
Totals			( )		( )

Chapter 25, P 4. (Continued)

Possible Causes of Variances

    Direct materials price variance:

    Direct materials quantity variance:

    Direct labor rate variance:

    Direct labor efficiency variance:

    Controllable manufacturing overhead variance:

    Manufacturing overhead volume variance:

Note: Because of the large variances for direct materials and direct labor, an investigation should be made to determine whether the standards should be revised.

Chapter 25, P 5.

Unknown amounts computed

a. Total manufacturing overhead variance

Because both variances are favorable,

Total Manufacturing Overhead Variance	=	Controllable Manufacturing Overhead Variance + Manufacturing Overhead Volume Variance
	=	( ) + ( )
	=	( )

b. Total manufacturing overhead costs applied

Because the manufacturing overhead volume variance is favorable,

Total Manufacturing Overhead Applied	=	Flexible Budget Based on Standard Hours Allowed + Manufacturing Overhead Volume Variance
	=	[(x hours) +] +
	=	+
	=	

c. Total manufacturing overhead rate per machine hour

Total Manufacturing Overhead Rate	=	Total Manufacturing Overhead Costs Applied ÷ Standard Machine Hours Allowed
	=	÷ hours
	=	

Chapter 25, P 5. (Continued)

d. Standard fixed manufacturing overhead rate

Standard Fixed Manufacturing Overhead Rate	=	Total Manufacturing Overhead Rate − Standard Variable Manufacturing Overhead Rate
	=	−
	=	

e. Normal capacity in machine hours

Normal Capacity	=	Budgeted Fixed Manufacturing Overhead ÷ Standard Fixed Manufacturing Overhead Rate
	=	÷
	=	hours

f. Actual variable and fixed manufacturing overhead

Actual Variable and Fixed Manufacturing Overhead	=	Flexible Budget Based on Standard Hours Allowed − Favorable Controllable Manufacturing Overhead Variance
	=	−
	=	

Chapter 25, P 6.

1. Total standard direct materials cost per unit determined

Clock facing					
Company A	(	x	)		
Company B	(	x	)		
Total					
Clock hands					
Ajax Hardware, Inc.	(	per set)			
Time movement					
Company Q	(	x	)		
Company R	(	x	)		
Company S	(	x	)		
Total					
Spring assembly					
French company	(	x	)		
Total standard direct materials cost per unit					

2. Standard direct materials unit cost revised based on guaranteed purchase

Total standard unit cost of direct materials before change		
Less original cost of clock hands		
Plus new purchase price of clock hands		
(x)		
Total standard unit cost of direct materials		

3. Standard direct materials unit cost revised based on use of substandard spring assemblies

Total standard unit cost of direct materials before change		
Less original cost of assemblies		
Plus new cost of substandard assemblies		
(÷)		
Total standard unit cost of direct materials		

Chapter 25, P 7.

1. Direct materials price and quantity variances computed

Direct materials price variance:

	Direct Materials	
	Metal (pounds)	Wood (ounces)
Price difference		
Standard price		
Less actual price		
Difference in price	( )	( )

Direct Materials Price Variance = (Standard Price − Actual Price) x Actual Quantity

Metal

| | ( ) | x | | pounds | = | ( ) |

Wood

| | ( ) | x | | ounces | = | ( ) |

Direct materials quantity variance:

	Direct Materials	
	Metal (pounds)	Wood (ounces)
Quantity difference		
Standard quantity		
Less actual quantity used		
Difference in quantity	( )	( )

Direct Materials Quantity Variance = Standard Price x (Standard Quantity − Actual Quantity)

Metal

| | x | ( ) | = | ( ) |

Wood

| | x | ( ) | = | ( ) |

Chapter 25, P 7. (Continued)

Check:

	Standard price × standard quantity						*
	Less actual price × actual quantity						**
							( )
							( )***
*	Metal	(	×	)	=		
	Wood	(	×	)	=		
	Total						
**	Metal	(	×	)	=		
	Wood	(	×	)	=		
	Total						
***		( )					
		( )					
		( )					
		( )					
		( )					

Chapter 25, P 7. (Continued)

2. Direct labor rate and efficiency variances computed

Direct labor rate variance:

	Direct Labor	
	Molding	Trimming/Finishing
Rate difference		
Standard rate		
Less actual rate		
Difference in rate	( )	( )

Direct Labor Rate Variance = (Standard Rate − Actual Rate) x Actual Hours

Molding Department

( ) x   hours = ( )

Trimming/Finishing Department

( ) x   hours = ( )

Direct labor efficiency variance:

	Direct Labor	
	Molding	Trimming/Finishing
Efficiency difference		
Standard hours allowed		
Less actual hours		
Difference in hours	( )	( )

Direct Labor Efficiency Variance = Standard Price x (Standard Hours − Actual Hours)

Molding Department

   x ( ) = ( )

Trimming/Finishing Department

   x ( ) = ( )

Chapter 25, P 7. (Continued)

Check:					
Standard rate x standard hours allowed					*
Less actual rate x actual hours					**
Total direct labor variance					( )
Total direct labor rate and efficiency variances					( )***
* Molding	(	x	)	=	
Trimming/Finishing	(	x	)	=	
Total					
** Molding	(	x	)	=	
Trimming/Finishing	(	x	)	=	
Total					
***	( )				
	( )				
	( )				
	( )				
	( )				

Chapter 25, P 8.

1. Variances computed

a. Direct materials price variances

Chemicals

Standard price						
Less actual price	(	÷	ounces)			
Difference						( )

Direct Materials Price Variance = (Standard Price − Actual Price) × Actual Quantity

= ( ) × ounces

= ( )

Packages

Standard price				
Less actual price	(	÷	packages)	
Difference				

Direct Materials Price Variance = (Standard Price − Actual Price) × Actual Quantity

= × packages

=

Chapter 25, P 8. (Continued)

b. Direct materials quantity variances

Chemicals

Standard quantity	(	packages	x	ounces)			
Less actual quantity							
Difference						( )	

Direct Materials Quantity Variance = Standard Price x (Standard Quantity − Actual Quantity)

= _____ per ounce x _____ ounces ( )
= _____ ( )

Packages

Standard quantity		
Less actual quantity		
Difference		( )

Direct Materials Quantity Variance = Standard Price x (Standard Quantity − Actual Quantity)

= _____ per package x _____ packages ( )
= _____ ( )

Check:

Standard cost for chemicals
_____ x (_____ packages x _____ ounces)
Less total actual chemicals costs
Net direct materials variance ( )
Total variances: ( ) + ( ) ( )
Standard cost for packaging
_____ x (_____ x _____)
Less total actual packaging costs
Net direct materials variance ( )
Total variances: _____ + ( ) ( )

Chapter 25, P 8. (Continued)

c. Direct labor rate variance

Standard rate					
Less actual rate	(	÷	hours)		
Difference in rate					( )

Direct Labor Rate Variance = (Standard Rate − Actual Rate) × Actual Hours
= ( ) × hours
= ( )

d. Direct labor efficiency variance

Standard hours allowed (packages × hour per package)

Less actual hours
Difference ( )

Direct Labor Efficiency Variance = Standard Rate × (Standard Hours Allowed − Actual Hours)
= (×) ( )
= ( )

Check:

Standard direct labor cost (× packages × hour per package)

Less actual direct labor cost
Net direct labor variance ( )
Total variances: ( ) + ( ) ( )

e. Controllable manufacturing overhead variance

Budgeted manufacturing overhead (flexible budget) for 50,000 packages:

Variable manufacturing overhead cost
(per hour × packages × hour per package)
Budgeted fixed manufacturing overhead cost
Total budgeted manufacturing overhead
Less actual manufacturing overhead costs incurred
(+)
Controllable manufacturing overhead variance ( )

Chapter 25, P 8. (Continued)

f.	Manufacturing overhead volume variance							
	Standard manufacturing overhead applied							
	[	packages x		hour x (		+	)]	
	Less total budgeted manufacturing overhead (see part e)							
	Manufacturing overhead volume variance							( )
	Check:							
	Actual manufacturing overhead incurred							
	Manufacturing overhead applied							
	Net manufacturing overhead variance							( )
	Controllable manufacturing overhead variance							( )
	Manufacturing overhead volume variance							( )
	Total manufacturing overhead cost variance							( )

Chapter 25, P 8. (Continued)

2. Performance report prepared

Lutz Laboratories, Inc.
Production Performance and Cost Variance Report
Product: Cold-Gone
For the First Week of April 20x3

Productivity Summary

| Normal capacity | _____ units |
| Good units produced | _____ units |

Cost and Variance Analysis

	Standard Cost	Actual Cost Incurred	Total Variance	Variance Breakdown Amount	Type
Direct materials:					
Chemicals			( )	( )	Direct materials price variance
				( )	Direct materials quantity variance
Packages			( )	( )	Direct materials price variance
				( )	Direct materials quantity variance
Direct labor			( )	( )	Direct labor rate variance
				( )	Direct labor efficiency variance
Manufacturing overhead			( )	( )	Controllable manufacturing overhead variance
				( )	Manufacturing overhead volume variance
Totals			( )	( )	

Chapter 25, P 8. (Continued)

Possible Causes of Variances

    Direct materials price variance:

    Direct materials quantity variance:

    Direct labor rate variance:

    Direct labor efficiency variance:

    Controllable manufacturing overhead variance:

    Manufacturing overhead volume variance:

Note: Several unfavorable variances that are controllable are obscured by the favorable manufacturing overhead volume variance (uncontrollable) and by the direct materials price variance.

Chapter 25, SD 5.

1. Standard hours allowed computed

Standard Hours Allowed	=	Good Units Produced × Standard Hours per Unit			
Policy developers					
Standard Hours Allowed	=	units	×	hours	
	=	hours			
Policy salespeople					
Standard Hours Allowed	=	units	×	hours	
	=	hours			

Chapter 25, SD 5. (Continued)

2. Total standard costs and actual costs computed

Standard costs for 265 units:							
Direct labor							
	Policy developers	(	x		hours	)	
	Policy salespeople	(	x		hours	)	
	Total direct labor cost						
Operating overhead							
	Variable operating overhead	(	x		units	)	
	Fixed operating overhead	(	x		units	)	
	Total operating overhead						
Total standard costs							
Actual costs for 265 units:							
Direct labor							
	Policy developers						
	Policy salespeople						
	Total direct labor cost						
Operating overhead							
	Variable operating overhead						
	Fixed operating overhead						
	Total operating overhead						
Total actual costs							
Total cost variance							
	(	–	)				( )

Chapter 25, SD 5. (Continued)

3. Direct labor variances computed

Direct Labor Rate Variance	=	(Standard Rate − Actual Rate) x Actual Hours		
Policy developers	=	(−	) x	hours
	=	( )		
Policy salespeople	=	(−	) x	hours
	=	( )		
Direct Labor Efficiency Variance	=	Standard Rate x (Standard Hours Allowed − Actual Hours)		
Policy developers		x (−	)	
	=	( )		
Policy salespeople		x (−	)	
	=			

Check:

Total standard direct labor cost		
Total actual direct labor cost		
Total direct labor variance		( )
Direct labor rate variances		
Developers		( )
Salespeople		( )
Direct labor efficiency variances		
Developers		( )
Salespeople		
Total direct labor variance		( )

Chapter 25, SD 5. (Continued)

4. Operating overhead variances computed

Total operating overhead variance									
	Standard operating overhead costs applied to units produced								
		total rate/hour	x	units produced	x	std hours/unit			
				x		x			
	Less actual operating overhead costs incurred								
	Total operating overhead variance								( )
Controllable operating overhead variance									
	Budgeted operating overhead (flexible budget) for 265 units:								
		Variable operating overhead cost							
			rate/hour	x	units	x	hours/unit		
				x		x			
	Budgeted fixed operating overhead cost								
	Total budgeted operating overhead								
	Less actual operating overhead costs incurred								
	Controllable operating overhead variance								( )
Operating overhead volume variance									
	Standard operating overhead applied								
		total rate/hour	x	units produced	x	std hours/unit			
				x		x			
	Less total budgeted operating overhead								
	Operating overhead volume variance								( )
Check:									
	Controllable operating overhead variance								( )
	Operating overhead volume variance								( )
	Total operating overhead variance								( )

Chapter 25, SD 5. (Continued)

5. Possible causes and solutions identified

Chapter 25, MRA 1.

1. Performance report analyzed using static budget

2. Budgeted selling fee and variable costs per home resale calculated

	Total for 180 Home Resales	Per Home Resale
Total selling fees		
Less variable costs		
Sales commissions		
Automobile		
Advertising		
Home repairs		
General overhead		

Chapter 25, MRA 1. (Continued)

3. Performance report using flexible budget prepared

<table>
<tr><td colspan="4">Boris Realtors, Inc.
Performance Report
For the Year Ended December 31, 20x5</td></tr>
<tr><td></td><td>Budget*</td><td>Actual**</td><td>Difference Under (Over) Budget</td></tr>
<tr><td>Total Selling Fees</td><td></td><td></td><td></td></tr>
<tr><td>Less Variable Costs</td><td></td><td></td><td></td></tr>
<tr><td>   Sales Commissions</td><td></td><td></td><td></td></tr>
<tr><td>   Automobile</td><td></td><td></td><td></td></tr>
<tr><td>   Advertising</td><td></td><td></td><td></td></tr>
<tr><td>   Home Repairs</td><td></td><td></td><td></td></tr>
<tr><td>   General Overhead</td><td></td><td></td><td></td></tr>
<tr><td>Less Fixed Costs</td><td></td><td></td><td></td></tr>
<tr><td>   General Overhead</td><td></td><td></td><td></td></tr>
<tr><td>Total Costs</td><td></td><td></td><td></td></tr>
<tr><td>Net Income</td><td></td><td></td><td></td></tr>
</table>

  * Budgeted data based on 200 home resales.
  ** Actual selling fees and operating costs of 200 home resales.

4. Performance report using flexible budget analyzed

5. Recommendations to improve next year's performance

Chapter 25, MRA 2.

1. a.

   b.

   c.

   d.

2. Variances calculated

Note: In this managerial reporting and analysis case, no items are produced or processed. Standard hours allowed differ from normal hours only when more or fewer items than normal are produced or processed. Therefore, in this case, the standard hours allowed for the month will equal normal hours, resulting in a zero value for the overhead volume variance.

Standard operating labor cost				
Actual operating labor cost				
Total operating labor variance				( )
Total Standard Hours	=	Normal Hours x Standard Number of Operators		
	=	x		
	=	hours		
Total Actual Hours	=	Actual Hours x Actual Number of Operators Used		
	=	x		
	=	hours		

Chapter 25, MRA 2. (Continued)

Operating Labor Rate Variance	=	(Standard Rate* − Actual Rate**) × Actual Hours		
	=	(−) ×		hours
	=	( )		
Operating Labor Efficiency Variance	=	Standard Rate × (Standard Hours Allowed − Actual Hours)		
	=	× (−)		
	=	( )		

Check:

Operating labor rate variance	( )
Operating labor efficiency variance	( )
Total operating labor variance	( )

*Standard Operating Labor Rate	=	Standard Operating Labor Cost ÷ Total Standard Hours
	=	÷
	=	per hour
**Actual Operating Labor Rate	=	Actual Operating Labor Cost ÷ Total Actual Hours
	=	÷
	=	per hour

Chapter 25, MRA 2. (Continued)

Controllable operating overhead variance computed

	Standard	Actual
Variable operating overhead costs		
Utilities costs		
Repairs and maintenance		
Total variable overhead costs		
Fixed operating overhead costs		
Depreciation, equipment		
Rent		
Other fixed operating overhead costs		
Total fixed operating overhead costs		
Total operating overhead costs		

Controllable Operating Overhead Variance = Total Standard Operating Overhead Cost − Actual Operating Overhead Costs Incurred

=   −

=   ( )

Chapter 25, MRA 2. (Continued)

3. Performance report prepared

<table>
<tr><td colspan="5" align="center">Forest Valley Spa
Performance Report
For the Month Ended March 31, 20x4</td></tr>
<tr><td></td><td colspan="2" align="center">Cost</td><td colspan="2" align="center">Variance</td></tr>
<tr><td></td><td>Standard</td><td>Actual</td><td>Amount</td><td>Type</td></tr>
<tr><td>Operating labor costs</td><td></td><td></td><td>( )</td><td>Labor rate variance</td></tr>
<tr><td></td><td></td><td></td><td>( )</td><td>Labor efficiency variance</td></tr>
<tr><td>Operating overhead costs</td><td></td><td></td><td>( )</td><td>Controllable overhead variance</td></tr>
<tr><td>Total costs</td><td></td><td></td><td>( )</td><td></td></tr>
</table>

Chapter 25, MRA 3.

The variances that could be affected:

a.

b.

c.

d.

e.

f.

g.

Chapter 25, MRA 4.

1. Flexible budget developed

FH Industries
Flexible Budget—Manufacturing Overhead
For an Average One-Month Period

Cost Category:	Machine Hours (MH) 2,000	2,200	2,500	Variable Cost per MH
Budgeted variable manufacturing overhead				
Indirect materials and supplies				
Indirect machine setup labor				
Materials handling				
Maintenance and repair				
Utilities				
Miscellaneous				
Total budgeted variable manufacturing overhead costs				
Budgeted fixed manufacturing overhead				
Supervisory salaries				
Machine depreciation				
Other				
Total budgeted fixed manufacturing overhead costs				
Total budgeted manufacturing overhead costs				

Chapter 25, MRA 4. (Continued)

2. Flexible budget formula formulated

Total Budgeted Manufac-turing Overhead Costs	=	(Variable Cost per Machine Hour x Number of MH) + Budgeted Fixed Manufacturing Overhead Costs
	=	(　　　　x Number of MH) +

3. Fixed costs per machine hour computed

Fixed Costs per Machine Hour	=	Budgeted Fixed Costs ÷ Normal Capacity in MH
	=	÷　　　　MH
	=	per MH

Detail of fixed manufacturing overhead rate:

Supervisory salaries	=		÷		MH	=
Machine depreciation	=		÷		MH	=
Other	=		÷		MH	=

Chapter 25, MRA 4. (Continued)

4. Comparative cost analysis prepared

Manufacturing Overhead Costs Applied
Based on 2,100 Standard Machine Hours Allowed

Cost Category	Cost per MH	Costs Applied	Actual Costs Incurred	Variance
Budgeted variable manufacturing overhead				
Indirect materials and supplies				( )
Indirect machine setup labor				( )
Materials handling				( )
Maintenance and repair				( )
Utilities				( )
Miscellaneous				( )
Total budgeted variable manufacturing overhead costs				( )
Budgeted fixed manufacturing overhead				
Supervisory salaries				( )
Machine depreciation				( )
Other				( )
Total budgeted fixed manufacturing overhead costs				( )
Total costs				( )

Chapter 25, MRA 4. (Continued)

5. Manufacturing overhead variance analysis developed

	Actual Manufacturing Overhead Costs Incurred	Flexible Budget at Level of Achieved Performance		Total Manufacturing Overhead Costs Applied	
Variable costs		x	=	x $7.40	=
Fixed costs		Budgeted fixed	=	x	=
Total					

Controllable Manufacturing Overhead Variance = ( )

Manufacturing Volume Variance = ( )

6. Analysis of variances prepared

1019

Chapter 26, SE 1.

1.
2.
3.
4.

Chapter 26, SE 2.

1.
2.
3.
4.
5.

Chapter 26, SE 3.

1.
2.
3.
4.
5.

Chapter 26, SE 4.

Performance Report for Cost Center C.

	Actual Costs	Variance	Flexible Budget	Variance	Master Budget
Units produced				( )	
Center costs					
Direct materials		( )		( )	
Direct labor		( )		( )	
Variable overhead		( )		( )	
Fixed overhead		( )			
Total cost		( )		( )	
Performance measures					
Defect-free units to total produced		( )	N/A		
Average throughput time per unit	minutes	minutes ( )	N/A		minutes

Chapter 26, SE 5.

Performance Report for Profit Center P.

	Master Budget	Actual Costs	Variance
Sales			( )
Controllable variable costs			
Variable cost of goods sold			( )
Variable selling and administrative			
expenses			( )
Contribution margin			
Controllable fixed costs			( )
Profit center income			( )
Performance measures			
Number of orders processed			( )
Average daily sales			( )
Number of units sold			( )

Chapter 26, SE 6.

	Subsidiary D	Subsidiary V
Total sales		
Operating income		
Average assets invested		
Profit margin		
Asset turnover	times	times
ROI		

Chapter 26, SE 7.

	Subsidiary J	Subsidiary K
Total sales		
Operating income		
Beginning assets invested		
Ending assets invested		
Average assets invested		
Profit margin		
Asset turnover	times	times
ROI		

Chapter 26, SE 8.

	Subsidiary H	Subsidiary F
Total sales		
Operating income		
Beginning assets invested		
Ending assets invested		
Average assets invested		
Desired ROI		
Residual income		

Chapter 26, SE 9.

	Subsidiary M	Subsidiary N
Total sales		
After-tax operating income		
Total assets		
Current liabilities		
Total assets − current liabilities		
Cost of capital		
Economic value added		

Chapter 26, SE 10.

Goal	Objective	Measure	Performance Target
Customer satisfaction			
Customer satisfaction			

Chapter 26, E 1.

1.		4.	
2.		5.	
3.		6.	

Chapter 26, E 2.

1.		4.	
2.		5.	
3.		6.	

Chapter 26, E 3.

1.
2.
3.
4.

Chapter 26, E 4.

1.
2.
3.
4.

Chapter 26, E 5.

1.
2.
3.
4.
5.
6.
7.
8.
9.
10.

Chapter 26, E 6.

1.
2.
3.
4.
5.
6.
7.
8.
9.
10.
11.

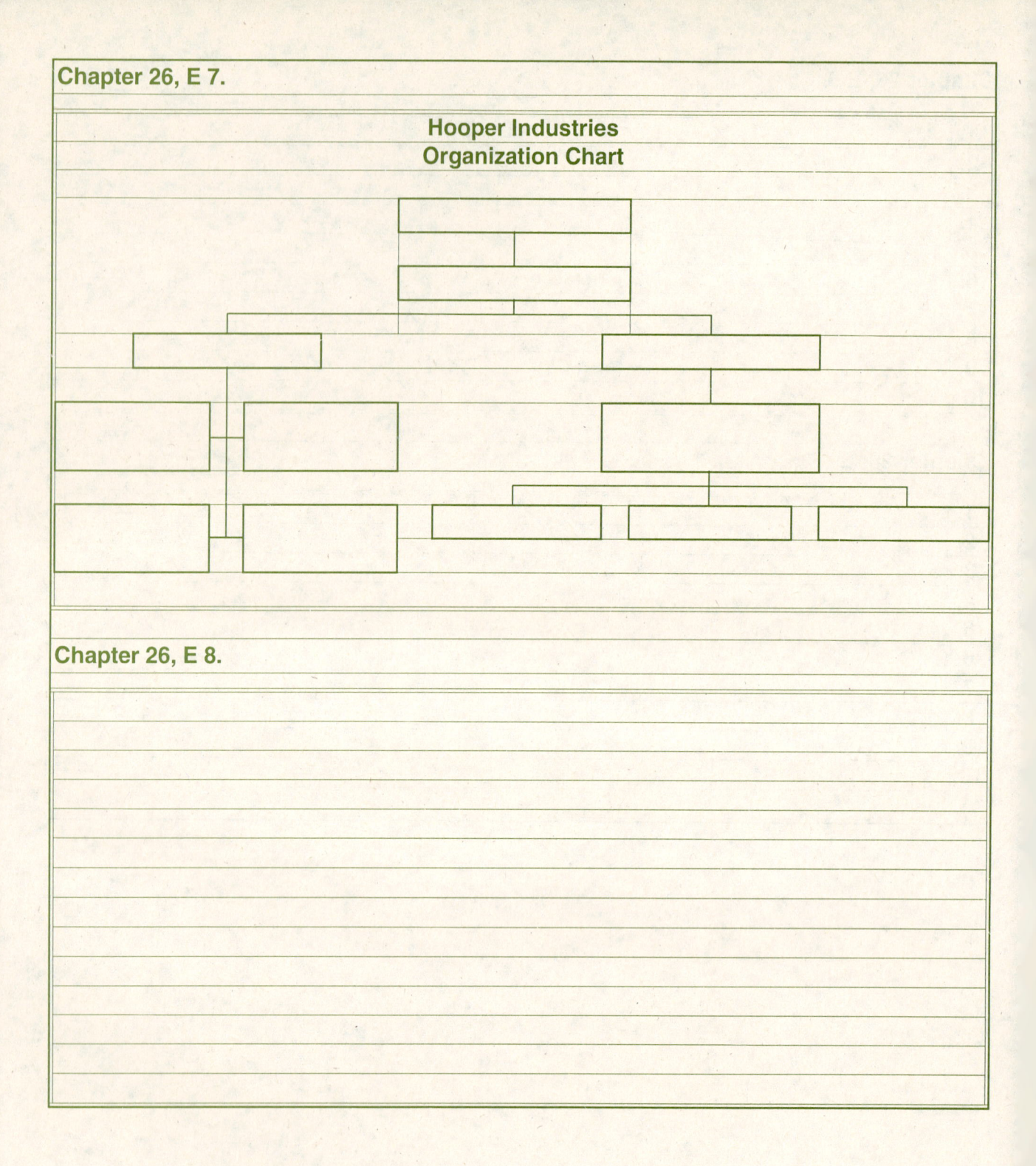

Chapter 26, E 7.

Hooper Industries
Organization Chart

Chapter 26, E 8.

Chapter 26, E 9.

	Master Budget	Actual Results	Variance
Sales			( )
Controllable variable costs			
Variable cost of goods sold			( )
Variable selling and administrative expenses			( )
Contribution margin			( )
Fixed costs			( )
Profit center income			( )
Performance measures			
Number of orders processed			( )
Average daily sales			( )

Chapter 26, E 10.

Bonsai Products, Inc.
Variable Costing Income Statement
For the Year Ended December 31, 20x3

Sales		
Controllable Variable Costs		
Variable Cost of Goods Sold		
Variable Selling Costs		
Contribution Margin		
Fixed Costs		
Fixed Manufacturing Costs		
Fixed Selling Expenses		
Fixed Administrative Expenses		
Profit Center Income		

Chapter 26, E 11.

	Actual Costs	Variance	Flexible Budget	Variance	Master Budget
Units produced					
Center costs					
Direct materials		( )			
Direct labor					
Variable overhead		( )			
Fixed overhead		( )			
Total cost		( )			
Performance measures					
Average daily pounds processed					
Average processing rate		( )			

Chapter 26, E 12.

	Glenn	Oaks
Sales		
Operating income		
Assets invested		
Desired ROI		
ROI		
Residual income		

Chapter 26, E 13.

	Lake	Sumpter	Poe
Sales			
After-tax operating income			
Total assets			
Current liabilities			
Cost of capital			
Total assets − current liabilities			
Economic value added			
Lake: − [( )] =			
Sumpter: − [( )] =			
Poe: − [( )] =			

Chapter 26, E 14.

Incentive	Effectiveness
Cash bonus	
Awards	
Profit sharing	
Stock options	

Chapter 26, E 15.

Goal: Company leads its industry in innovation

Perspective	Objective	Measure	Target
Financial (investors)			
Learning and growth (employees)			
Internal business processes			
Customers			

Chapter 26, P 1.

1. Performance report for East Coast plant prepared

	East Coast	Variance	Flexible Budget	Variance	Master Budget
Center costs					
Rolled aluminum	( )			( )	
Lids	( )			( )	
Direct labor	( )			( )	
Small tools and supplies	( )			( )	
Depreciation and rent					
Total cost		( )		( )	
Performance measures					
Cans processed per hour		( )			
Average daily pounds of scrap metal		( )			
Cans processed (in millions)				( )	

2. Performance report for West Coast plant prepared

	West Coast	Variance	Flexible Budget	Variance	Master Budget
Center costs					
Rolled aluminum	( )			( )	
Lids	( )			( )	
Direct labor	( )			( )	
Small tools and supplies	( )			( )	
Depreciation and rent					
Total cost		( )		( )	
Performance measures					
Cans processed per hour		( )			
Average daily pounds of scrap metal		( )			
Cans processed (in millions)				( )	

Chapter 26, P 1 (Continued)

3. Performance reports compared and discussed

Chapter 26, P 2.

1. Traditional income statement prepared

Zygo Corporation
Traditional Income Statement
For the Year Ended December 31, 20x4

Sales (		x	)	
Cost of Goods Sold				
Gross Margin				
Selling and Administrative Expenses				
Variable Selling Expenses				
Fixed Selling Expenses				
Fixed Administrative Expenses				
Center Income				

2. Variable costing income statement prepared

Zygo Corporation
Variable Costing Income Statement
For the Year Ended December 31, 20x4

Sales (		x	)	
Controllable Variable Costs				
Variable Cost of Goods Sold				
Variable Selling Expenses				
Contribution Margin				
Controllable Fixed Costs				
Fixed Manufacturing Overhead				
Fixed Selling Expenses				
Fixed Administrative Expenses				
Center Income				

Chapter 26, P 3.

1. Performance report for Seminole Branch prepared

Olin, Comfort, and Clark, LLP
Seminole Branch
Performance Report for Year Ended December 31, 20x4

Partner in Charge: Victoria Luna

	Actual Results	Variance	Flexible Budget	Variance	Master Budget
Billed hours					
Revenue		( )		( )	
Controllable variable costs					
Direct labor		( )			
Variable overhead		( )		( )	
Contribution margin		( )		( )	
Controllable fixed costs					
Rent					
Other administrative expenses		( )			
Branch operating income				( )	

Chapter 26, P 3. (Continued)

2. Performance report discussed

3a. ROI and RI of Seminole Branch computed

	Actual	Flexible	Master
ROI	= ( ) ÷	= ( ) ÷	= ( ) ÷
Residual income	= – (×)	= – (×)	= – (×)

3b. ROI and RI of Seminole Branch discussed

Chapter 26, P 4.

1. Division profit margin, asset turnover, and return on investment for 20x4 and 20x3 computed

	20x4			20x3	
Profit margin	÷	=	÷	=	
Asset turnover	÷ [(+) ÷]	=	÷ [(+) ÷]	=	
Return on investment			=			=

2. Division residual income for 20x4 and 20x3 computed

	20x4			20x3	
Residual income	− [(+) ÷]	=	− [(+) ÷]	=

3. Division economic value added for 20x4 and 20x3 computed

	20x4			20x3	
Economic value added	− (−) − (−) ÷	=	− (−) − (−) ÷	=

Chapter 26, P 5.

1. ___ − [(___ + ___) ÷ ___] = ___

2. a. ___ ÷ ___ = ___
    b. ___ ÷ [(___ + ___) ÷ ___] = ___ times
    c. ___ ÷ [(___ + ___) ÷ ___] = ___
    or
    ___ x 2

3. a. ___ ÷ [(___ + ___) ÷ ___] = ___
    b. ___ ÷ [(___ + ___) ÷ ___] = ___
    c. ___ ÷ [(___ + ___) ÷ ___] = ___

4. ___ − [(___ − ___)] = ___

Chapter 26, P 6.

1. Traditional income statement prepared

Sierra Mills, Inc.
Traditional Income Statement
For the Month Ended March 31, 20x5

Sales	
Cost of Goods Sold	
Gross Margin	
Selling and Administrative Expenses	
Variable Selling Expenses	
Fixed Selling Expenses	
Fixed General and Administrative Expenses	
Profit Center Income	

2. Variable costing income statement prepared

Sierra Mills, Inc.
Variable Costing Income Statement
For the Month Ended March 31, 20x5

Sales	
Controllable Variable Costs	
Variable Cost of Goods Sold	
Variable Selling Expenses	
Contribution Margin	
Fixed Costs	
Fixed Manufacturing Overhead	
Fixed Selling Expenses	
Fixed General and Administrative Expenses	
Profit Center Income	

Chapter 26, P 7.

1. Performance report for Highlands Theater prepared

Highlands Theater
Performance Report for the Month

Manager: Anne Burgman

	Actual Results	Variance	Flexible Budget	Variance	Master Budget
Tickets sold					
Revenue—tickets		( )		( )	
Revenue—concessions		( )		( )	
Total revenue				( )	
Controllable variable costs					
Concessions		( )		( )	
Direct labor		( )		( )	
Variable overhead		( )		( )	
Contribution margin					
Controllable fixed costs					
Rent					
Other administrative expenses		( )			
Theater operating income					( )

Chapter 26, P 7. (Continued)

2. Performance report discussed

3a. ROI and RI of Highlands Theater computed

	Actual	Flexible	Master
ROI	= ÷	= ÷	= ÷
Residual income	= − (×)	= − (×)	= − (×)

3b. ROI and RI discussed

Chapter 26, P 8.

1.   − [(+   ) ÷   ] =

2. a.   ÷   =
   b.   ÷ [(+   ) ÷   ] = times
   c.   ÷ [(+   ) ÷   ] =

   or

      x

3.   − [(−   )] =

Chapter 26, MRA 4.

1. Data entered and actual ROI and RI calculated

Investment Center	Food and Lodging Division
	Actual Results
Sales	
Operating income	
Average assets invested	
Desired ROI	
Return on Investment	
Profit Margin	
Asset Turnover	times
Residual Income	

2. ROI and RI calculated: desired ROI = 40%; invested assets = $10,000,000

Investment Center	Food and Lodging Division
	Actual Results
Sales	
Operating income	
Average assets invested	
Desired ROI	
Return on Investment	
Profit Margin	
Asset Turnover	times
Residual Income	

Chapter 26, MRA 4. (Continued)

3. ROI and RI calculated: desired ROI = 30%; invested assets = $12,000,000

Investment Center	Food and Lodging Division
	Actual Results
Sales	
Operating income	
Average assets invested	
Desired ROI	
Return on Investment	
Profit Margin	
Asset Turnover	
Residual Income	

4.

Chapter 27, SE 1.

1.
2.
3.
4.
5.

Chapter 27, SE 2.

Fonseca Corporation
Incremental Analysis

	Harvey Machine	Vogle Machine	Difference in Favor of Vogle Machine
Increase in revenues			
Increase in annual operating costs			
Direct labor			
Variable manufacturing overhead			
Total increase in operating costs			
Resulting change in operating income			

Chapter 27, SE 3.

Zorich Company
Make-or-Buy Decision
Incremental Analysis

	Make Part 23X	Buy Part 23X	Difference in Favor of Make
Costs to make the part			
Direct materials			
(x $3.50)			
Direct labor			
(x)			
Variable manufacturing overhead			
(x)			
Costs to buy the part			
(x)			
(x)			
Totals			

Because Zorich Company will save _____ by making the part, it should do so.

Note: Variable selling costs are irrelevant to this decision because they would be the same under either alternative.

Chapter 27, SE 4.

Net Gain (Loss)	=	(Unit Selling Price − Unit Variable Manufacturing Costs) x Units
	=	[− (+ +)] x Units
	=	x Units
	=	

Chapter 27, SE 5.

Perez Industries
Sell or Process-Further Decision
Incremental Analysis

(1)	Revenue if sold at split-off		per unit
(2)	Revenue if processed further		per unit
(3)	Incremental revenue (2 − 1)		per unit
(4)	Incremental costs		per unit
(5)	Increase in operating income if processed further (3 − 4)		per unit

Note: The joint costs are irrelevant because they are incurred regardless of the point at which the products are sold.

Chapter 27, SE 6.

Chapter 27, SE 7.

	x	*	=	

*Table 4 in the appendix on future value and present value tables.

Chapter 27, SE 8.

Net Present Value	=	Present Value of Future Net Cash Inflows − Cost of Equipment
	=	(× *) −
	=	−
	=	

*Table 4 in the appendix on future value and present value tables.

Chapter 27, SE 9.

$$\text{Average Investment Cost} = \frac{\text{Total Investment} - \text{Residual Value}}{2} + \text{Residual Value}$$

$$\text{Average Investment Cost} = \frac{\underline{\qquad} - \underline{\qquad}}{\underline{\qquad}} + \underline{\qquad} = \underline{\qquad}$$

$$\text{Accounting Rate of Return} = \frac{\text{Project's Average Annual Net Income}}{\text{Average Investment Cost}}$$

$$\text{Accounting Rate of Return} = \frac{\underline{\qquad}}{\underline{\qquad}} = \underline{\qquad}$$

Chapter 27, SE 10.

Payback Period	=	Cost of Equipment ÷ Annual Net Cash Inflows
	=	÷
	=	years

Chapter 27, E 1.

a.
b.
c.
d.
e.

Chapter 27, E 2.

1. Relevant data identified

2. Analysis prepared

Chesney Industries
Incremental Analysis

	Model A	Model B	Difference in Favor of Model B
Increase in cost savings			
Increase in operating costs			
Computer and software rental			
Desk rental			
Training costs			
Total increase in operating costs			
Resulting change in operating income			

Chapter 27, E 3.

Retoric Audio Systems, Inc.
Make-or-Buy Decision
Incremental Analysis

	Make	Buy	Difference in Favor of Make
Direct materials			
(x)			
Direct labor			
(x)			
Variable manufacturing overhead			
(x)			
To purchase parts			
(÷ 100 x)			
Totals			

Note: The solution does not include fixed costs in the totals because they are the same under both alternatives and therefore are irrelevant to the analysis.

Chapter 27, E 4.

Olga Antiquities, Ltd.
Special Order Decision
Contribution Margin Analysis

	Without Special Order (20,000 shades)	With Special Order (21,000 shades)
Sales		
(____ × ____)		
(____ × ____) + (____ × ____)		
Less variable costs		
Direct materials (____ per shade)		
Direct labor (____ per shade)		
Variable manufacturing overhead		
(____ × ____)		
Shipping (____ per shade)		
Total variable costs		
Contribution margin		

Note: This amount is verified by the following computation:

Net Gain = (Unit Selling Price − Variable Manufacturing Costs) × Units
= (____ − ____) × ____ Shades
= ____ × ____ Shades
= ____

Chapter 27, E 5.

1. Quantities to be produced computed

Brunner, Inc.
Product Mix Decision
Contribution Margin Analysis

	Product A	Product M
Selling price per unit		
Less variable cost per unit		
Contribution margin per unit		
Machine hours (MH) per unit		
Contribution margin per MH		
Labor hours (LH) per unit		
Contribution margin per LH		

2. Contribution margin for total product volume computed

Sales	(	x	)	
Variable costs	(	x	)	
Contribution margin				

Chapter 27, E 6.

Quality Meats
Sell or Process-Further Decision
Incremental Analysis

	Ham	Turkey
Revenue if sold at split-off		
Revenue if processed further		
Incremental revenue		
Incremental costs		
Operating income from further processing		

Chapter 27, E 7.

1. From Table 4 in the appendix on future value and present value tables:

		×		=	

2. From Table 3 in the appendix on future value and present value tables:

		×		=	

3. From Table 3 in the appendix on future value and present value tables:

			×		=	
			×		=	
			×		=	
			×		=	
	Total					

4. From Table 4 in the appendix on future value and present value tables:

		×		=	

5. From Table 3 in the appendix on future value and present value tables:

Year	1		×		=	
	2		×		=	
	3		×		=	
	4		×		=	
	5		×		=	
Total						

6. From Table 3 in the appendix on future value and present value tables:

Use year 6 factor (end of year 6 = beginning of year 7)

		×		=	

Chapter 27, E 8.

1. Net present value of each alternative computed

Machine N

Year		Net Cash Inflows	12% Factor*	Present Value	
1					
2					
3					
4					
5					
6					
7					
8					
9					
10					
Residual value					
Net present value					

*Table 3 in the appendix on future value and present value tables.

Machine O

Present value of ten equal annual net cash inflows of		each		*	
Residual value				**	
Net present value					

*Table 4 in the appendix on future value and present value tables.
**Table 3 in the appendix on future value and present value tables.

2. Purchase recommended

Chapter 27, E 9.

Year		Net Cash Inflows	14% Factor	Present Value
1–10			*	
	Residual value		**	
Total present value of cash inflows				
Less purchase price of machine				
Net present value				

* Table 4 in the appendix on future value and present value tables.
** Table 3 in the appendix on future value and present value tables.

Chapter 27, E 10.

Using Table 3 in the appendix on future value and present value tables:

Year	Net Cash Inflows	x	14% Factor	=	Present Value
1					
2					
3					
4					
5					
6					
Total present value					
Cost of initial investment					
Positive net present value					

A quicker way to arrive at the total present value using Table 4 in the appendix on future value and present value tables is as follows:

Total present value		x		=	
Less purchase price of machine					
Positive net present value					

Note: The difference between the total present value using Table 4 and Table 3 is $57.50 ($223,617.50 − $223,560.00). The difference exists because the numbers in the tables have been rounded. Regardless of the table used, the decision is the same—the machine should be purchased.

Chapter 27, E 11.

Average Investment	=	(	−	)	+		=	
Project's Average Annual Net Income	=		−		=			
Accounting Rate of Return	=		=					

Chapter 27, E 12.

$$\text{Payback Period} = \frac{\text{Cost of Machine}}{\text{Cash Revenue} - \text{Cash Expenses}}$$

=

=

= _____ years

Chapter 27, P 1.

1. Incremental analysis prepared

Iron Refrigerator Company
Make-or-Buy Decision
Incremental Analysis

	Make	Buy	Difference in Favor of Make
Direct materials			
x			
Direct labor			
(÷ 6) x			
Variable manufacturing overhead			
x			
To purchase completed clocks			
x (÷ x)			
Totals			

Note: Depreciation and other fixed manufacturing overhead remain the same for both alternatives and, therefore, are irrelevant to the analysis.

Chapter 27, P 1. (Continued)

2. Unit costs computed

To make				
Direct materials				
Direct labor				
	÷			
Variable manufacturing overhead				
Fixed manufacturing overhead				
	÷			*
Total unit cost				
To buy				
Purchase price				
(	÷	12	)	
Fixed manufacturing overhead				
	÷			*
Total unit cost				
*Rounded.				
Check:				
(	−	) x	clocks =	
(see part 1)				

Chapter 27, P 2.

Incremental analysis prepared

Barca Industries
Special Order Decision
Incremental Analysis

Special Order

   Sales

      (_____ boats @ _____ per boat)

   Less variable costs

      Direct materials

         [(_____ aluminum sheets @ _____) x _____]

      Direct labor

         [(_____ hours @ _____) x _____]

      Variable manufacturing overhead

         [(_____ hours @ _____) x _____]

      Total variable costs

   Contribution margin

Chapter 23, P 3.

1. Relevant costs and revenues identified

The expansion of product offerings would be made based on:

	Relevant Revenue	Relevant Costs	Incremental Contribution Margin
Bagels with cream cheese			
Bagel sandwiches			

2. Expansion discussed

3. Incremental analysis performed

All-Bagels, Inc.
Sell or Process-Further Decision
Incremental Analysis

Incremental revenue if processed further:	Bagels with Cream Cheese	Bagel Sandwiches
Process further		
Split-off		
Incremental revenue		
Less Incremental costs		
Operating income from further processing		

Chapter 27, P 4.

1. Net present value method applied to purchase of machine, 14% rate of return

Year		Net Cash Inflows	14% Factor	Present Value	
1–15			*		
	Residual value		**		
Total present value of cash inflows					
Less purchase price of machine					
Net present value					

* Table 4 in the appendix on future value and present value tables.
** Table 3 in the appendix on future value and present value tables.

2. Net present value method applied to purchase of machine, 16% rate of return

Year		Net Cash Inflows	16% Factor	Present Value	
1–15			*		
	Residual value		**		
Total present value of cash inflows					
Less purchase price of machine					
Net present value					

* Table 4 in the appendix on future value and present value tables.
** Table 3 in the appendix on future value and present value tables.

Chapter 24, P 5.

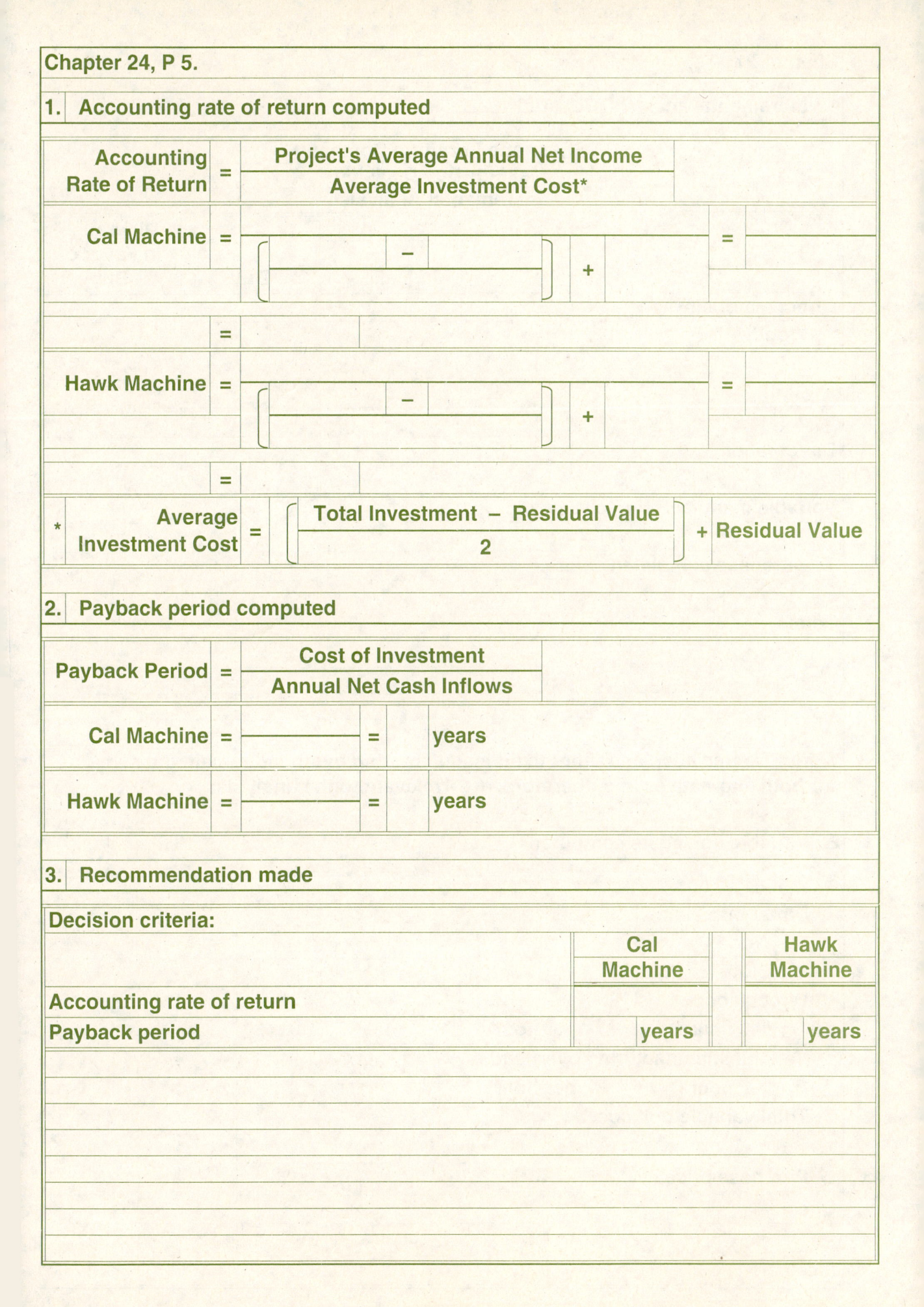

1. Accounting rate of return computed

$$\text{Accounting Rate of Return} = \frac{\text{Project's Average Annual Net Income}}{\text{Average Investment Cost*}}$$

Cal Machine = (___ − ___) + ___ = ___

= ___

Hawk Machine = (___ − ___) + ___ = ___

= ___

* $\text{Average Investment Cost} = \left(\dfrac{\text{Total Investment} - \text{Residual Value}}{2}\right) + \text{Residual Value}$

2. Payback period computed

$$\text{Payback Period} = \frac{\text{Cost of Investment}}{\text{Annual Net Cash Inflows}}$$

Cal Machine = ___ = ___ years

Hawk Machine = ___ = ___ years

3. Recommendation made

Decision criteria:	Cal Machine	Hawk Machine
Accounting rate of return		
Payback period	___ years	___ years

Chapter 27, P 6.

1. Incremental analysis prepared

Shoshone Furniture Company
Make-or-Buy Decision
Incremental Analysis

	Make	Buy	Difference in Favor of Buy
Direct materials			
Wood			
(x)			
Cloth			
(x)			
Direct labor			
x x			
Variable manufacturing overhead			
x x			
To purchase completed chairs			
x			
Totals			

Note: Depreciation and other fixed manufacturing overhead remain the same for both alternatives and, therefore, are irrelevant to the analysis.

2. Variable unit costs computed

To make
- Direct materials
  - Wood
  - Cloth
- Direct labor
  - (hours x   per hour)
- Variable manufacturing overhead
  - (hours x   per hour)
- Total variable unit cost

To buy
- Purchase price   (÷   )

Check:
(−   ) x   chairs
(see part 1)

Chapter 27, P 7.

1. Net present value method applied to purchase of machine, 12% rate of return

Year		Net Cash Inflows	12% Factor	Present Value
1–12			*	
	Residual value		**	
Total present value of cash inflows				
Less purchase price of machine				
Net present value				

The machine will yield more than a 12 percent rate of return, so management should purchase the machine.

2. Net present value method applied to purchase of machine, 14% rate of return

Year		Net Cash Inflows	14% Factor	Present Value
1–12			*	
	Residual value		**	
Total present value of cash inflows				
Less purchase price of machine				
Net present value				

* Table 4 in the appendix on future value and present value tables.
** Table 3 in the appendix on future value and present value tables.

Chapter 27, P 8.

1. Net present value computed

Exalt Machine

Year		Net Cash Inflows	16% Factor	Present Value	
1–10			*		
	Residual value		**		
Total present value of cash inflows					
Less cost of Exalt Machine					
Net present value					

Landis Machine

Year		Net Cash Inflows	16% Factor	Present Value	
1–10			*		
	Residual value		**		
Total present value of cash inflows					
Less cost of Landis Machine					
Net present value					

* Table 4 in the appendix on future value and present value tables.
** Table 3 in the appendix on future value and present value tables.

Chapter 27, P 8. (Continued)

2. Accounting rate of return computed

$$\text{Accounting Rate of Return} = \frac{\text{Project's Average Annual Net Income}}{\text{Average Investment Cost*}}$$

Exalt Machine = ((___ − ___) + ___) = ___

= ___

Landis Machine = ((___ − ___) + ___) = ___

= ___

* $\text{Average Investment Cost} = \left(\dfrac{\text{Total Investment} - \text{Residual Value}}{2}\right) + \text{Residual Value}$

3. Payback period computed

$$\text{Payback Period} = \frac{\text{Cost of Investment}}{\text{Annual Net Cash Inflows}}$$

Exalt Machine = ___ = ___ years

Landis Machine = ___ = ___ years

4. Recommendation made

Decision criteria:

	Exalt Machine	Landis Machine
Net present value		
Accounting rate of return		
Payback period	years	years

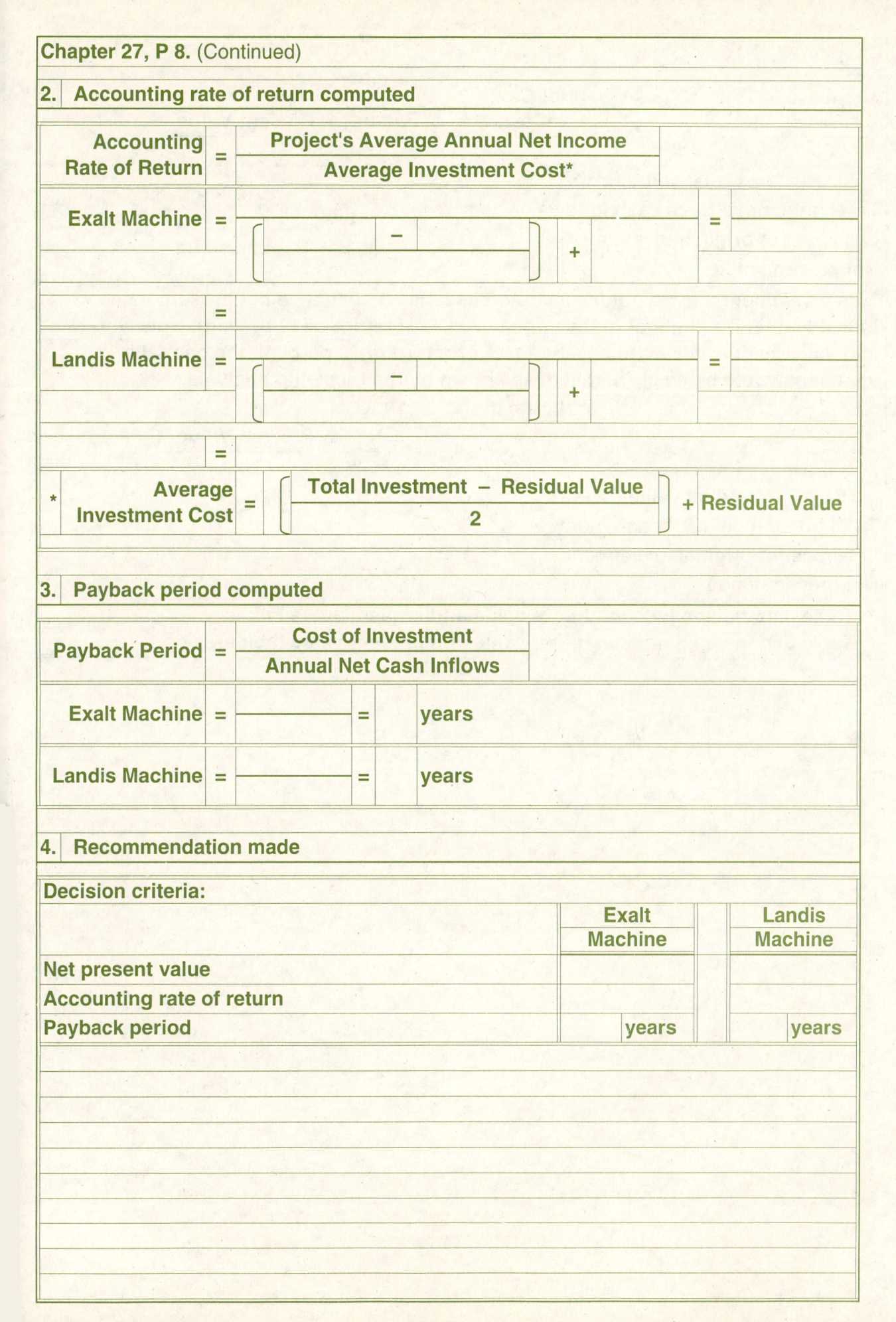

Chapter 27, SD 5.

Years		Net Cash Inflows	12% Factor	Present Value
1–20			*	
20	(residual value)		**	
Total present value of cash inflows				
Less cost of original investment				
Net present value				

This investment should not be accepted because its negative net present value indicates that it will not earn the minimum rate of return of 12 percent. However, if management is willing to accept a rate of return of 10 percent, the capital investment would be easily justified, as shown by the following analysis.

Years		Net Cash Inflows	10% Factor	Present Value
1–20			*	
20	(residual value)		**	
Total present value of cash inflows				
Less cost of original investment				
Net present value				

* Table 4 in the appendix on future value and present value tables.
** Table 3 in the appendix on future value and present value tables.

Chapter 27, MRA 1.

1. Profitability of special orders analyzed

Roscoe Can Opener Company
Special Order Decision
Contribution Margin Analysis

	Order 1	Order 2	Order 3
Sales			
Less variable costs			
Direct materials			
Direct labor			
Variable overhead			
Packaging			
Total variable costs			
Contribution margin			

2. Order selected